# WITHOUT
# FEAR

A SOLDIER'S MEMOIR OF
SACRIFICE, LOVE, TRAGEDY, AND TRIUMPH
IN CENTRAL IRAQ

## WALTER L. ROSADO

2017

Cover Design by Kerry Hynds, *Aero Gallerie*—Copyright © 2017 by Walter L. Rosado

Interior Design by Colleen Sheehan, *Write Dream Repeat Book Interior Design*—Copyright © 2017 by Walter L. Rosado

Published via CreateSpace Independent Publishing Platform. CreateSpace is a registered trademark of Amazon.Com, Inc.

ISBN-13: 978-1544665870
ISBN-10: 1544665873

First Edition, May 2017

Pittsburgh, PA USA

*Dedicated to the past, present, and future soldiers
of the 28TH Infantry Division.*

# MAP

*"The secret of all victory lies in the organization of the non-obvious."*

—Marcus Aurelius
(Roman Emperor 121-180 b.c.)

# CONTENTS

# ACKNOWLEGEMENTS

MANY PEOPLE CONTRIBUTED to bringing this book to print in its current form.

I would like to thank all of the men and women that served with me in the military. There are too many of you to list than space and time allows, however I would like to specifically call out the men that were in my section during my deployment to Iraq.

*Benjamin Smith*
*Thomas Anderson*
*Matthew Fassette*
*Justin Adamowicz*
*Brad McDonald*
*Charles Pearson*
*Richard Griffiths*
*Michael Sullivan*
*Tony Reitz*
*Maurice Jasper*

I would like to thank those who acted as editors or beta readers:

*Kristin Antosz*
*Melissa Survinski*
*Barbara Ford*
*Christine File*

I would like to thank my family for their undying support:

*Rusty Rosado*
*Suzanne Rosado*
*Nancy Stauffer*
*Russell Beeghly*

I would also like to thank the hundreds of people who united around social media to support this book, pushing me to complete it. Without you these thoughts would have stayed in a spiral notebook on a dusty bookshelf. I wrote Without Fear in 2009. It was a diary—nothing more. It took eight years to make it public. It was difficult for me to open up and share such intimate details about my life and my time in Iraq. I'm not sure that I would have had the confidence to follow through with it if it weren't for so many people showing such strong interest in my story.

Last, but certainly not least, I want to thank God. I can do all things through him who gives me strength.

# INTRODUCTION

**W**E LIVE IN A TIME of perpetual war. Acts of terror have become commonplace in a globally connected world. Socio-economic uncertainty and geopolitical realities demand efficient, effective, and proactive military dominance in an age where the lines between good and evil are sometimes hard to define. This isn't your typical book about war. In fact, it is in many ways the opposite. An Army recruiting commercial showing men jumping out of airplanes, rappelling from a helicopter, ascending from swamp in scuba gear, and charging up a hill towards a heavily fortified enemy position with rifles drawn largely inspired this book. Though these are all things that soldiers do in fact do, only the combat elite actually engage in these activities on a regular basis, and even then those activities would represent only a small fraction of what deployed soldiers do. The commercial, though effective at aiding recruiting efforts, and the current narrative that most American civilians believe about their soldiers abroad is dishonest.

When I found out that I was deploying to Iraq as a Human Resources Specialist in an infantry regiment, I saw an opportunity to capture my experience in writing and tell the truth about what life as a soldier was like. My purpose was not to call out the U.S. for a dishonest narrative of what military life encompasses, but rather to highlight what life is actually like for a run of the mill average soldier. This is my story, and the story of the men with which I served. This book is about regular soldiers in irregular situations, and the all too familiar experiences of missing home, goofing off, and soldiers doing their jobs to the best of their abilities.

# BEFORE THE ARMY

I WAS BORN AND RAISED in Pittsburgh, Pennsylvania. My parents were both disabled. My mother, Suzanne, was deaf and suffered from seizures. My father, Luis, was absent for most of my life. I never really knew him, but I did know his rage. He would beat my mother and I regularly.

I was born into extreme poverty. My family didn't have any money. As an infant, a close brush with meningitis very nearly took my life. The doctors said I should have died. They felt that I might have brain damage, or worse. I was fortunate that the physicians were wrong. The doctors called me a "fighter". The odds were stacked against me in every way. My parents did their best, but it wasn't enough. For the first five years of my life, I felt like more a tool for my deaf parents than a child. I had to order food, deal with phone calls, bills, and much more. It was difficult to be the child of people that couldn't hear. It really never felt fair. I was never free. I was always sad, even when I was smiling. Still to this day, I feel that depression engrained into my soul. The physical and verbal abuse molded me into a child with low self-esteem, abandonment issues, and an eating disorder. When people told me that I could do anything and be anything that I strived for because I was an American I didn't believe them. I was a reluctant member of the so-called "trophy generation".

My life started to change when my younger brother was born. People seemed to be genuinely concerned that he would have to deal with the same hardships that I did. To the court system, a series of unfortunate events served as a signal that my parents were not fit to care for me or my brother Rusty. Grandma swept in to rescue us both, and after several court battles, succeeded, winning full custody. This improved my life a million fold. No one saw potential in me except for my grandmother. She made sure that I had tutors, music lessons, and could play sports. Grandma often worked odd jobs trying to provide enough for all of us to get by. I hated all the jobs she had. Even though things seemed to be getting immeasurably better, I still often felt like I was all alone.

I first decided I would join the military when I was in elementary school. My cousin had served aboard the U.S.S. Abraham Lincoln during the Gulf War Conflict and I had a deep respect for the veterans in the American Legion post that I saw marching in all of my small suburban community's parades. Even as a fourth-grader, I knew that I wanted to matter, maybe because I felt like I did not. I wanted to be a part of a team that made a difference, to take part in an epic campaign against the bad guys. I loved my county; I wanted to wear the uniform.

In sixth grade, I tried to drop out of junior high school and enlist. In the bone-chilling winter, I made it from my home to the recruiting office five miles away—on foot—only to be given a ride home and be told by a Captain that the better educated I was before joining the military the better I could serve and the farther I could go. This notion and my aspirations for a military career were the only reasons that I was motivated to do well in school.

My high school years were rough. Despite my best efforts, my grades suffered. I tried to be active in some extracurriculars and was on the wrestling team and in the orchestra. Being poor in Fox Chapel, which was at the time the wealthiest public school district in the state, presented challenges. I didn't have many friends aside from two kids I got along well enough with, but they both came from families that were very well off. Wealth was something that I looked at in an interesting way. I saw myself as being stronger for having less but at the same time wanted more. There were many challenges associated with my notion of wealth that may not have had a direct impact on my military career, but it most certainly molded me into the type of person for whom the military was very attractive to. In the Army I saw a potential escape route from a life on the streets. I was poor and would have never been taken seriously if it weren't for my own desire to one day serve my country. I never had a girlfriend. I learned major life lessons from failed attempts at running for both student council president and vice president of the Technology Student's Association. I fell short of many of my early academic and athletic goals, but I always kept going. I never quit; I always pushed forward.

On September 11, 2001, my country bled. Sitting in biology class, an eerie anxiety crept over the room as the students all knew something was going on, but not quite what. We were caught completely off guard. At first, our teacher was candid with us, yet brief. Perhaps she had limited knowledge of the events herself. She told us simply that a plane had crashed. Later, the teachers must have been encouraged to not discuss the event with us. My high school had strict policies against cell phone use and not surprisingly, a huge line was building up at the gym and auditorium's pay phones, so information was incomplete. Students had no clue what was going on and it scared them. Yet gym class was relatively normal; we all changed into our shorts, t-shirts, and sneakers but we didn't work out that day. But it was in gym class that a message came over the school loud speaker announcement system: "Will the following students please report to the main office." Parents were pulling their children from school. Confusion reigned free. By the evening the pieces of the puzzle fell into place—our country had been attacked multiple times in a coordinated terrorist effort. At the Pentagon in our nation's capital, the strategic heart of the United States military; at the World Trade Center, reaping the most destruction that I had known in my lifetime; and in Somerset County, just sixty miles short of my hometown of Pittsburgh, but still too close to home. An unholy trinity.

What followed was sadness. There were so many dead, wounded, and missing. Many tried to compare the attack to Pearl Harbor, the opening volley of World War II, but the casualties in the 9/11 attacks were different, uniquely civilian. No one my age had ever seen or felt anything like it. Even though so many of us were miles away from Ground Zero, everyone knew someone who was impacted. Future generations won't feel the weight that 9/11 brought simply for those of us who witnessed the day's events, much less for those who were there.

Even then, there was no doubt that the enemy was representative of radical Islam—a religion, philosophy, economic stance, and military ideology all rolled up into one. A radical representation inherently opposed to the Western way of life. There were no arguments of political correctness or sensitivity as even American Muslims publicly demanded an immediate military response. American flags flew everywhere. Monuments were built, art and poetry were inked, and music was composed. The coming war would be a holy war, fought by crusaders and infidels.

Nobody wanted to admit it but the country of liberty, laws, and freedom was hungry for revenge. It was the responsibility of the government to oblige the citizens that request. They did. I cannot comment as to the "real" reasons for our war with Iraq or even Afghanistan. There will be theories and suspicions of malicious intent for many years to come. Our enemies' allegiances seemed to me to be with Saudi Arabia. There were 19 terrorist hijackers that carried out the 9/11 attack, all affiliated with al-Qaeda. Fifteen of the nineteen terrorists were citizens of the Kingdom of Saudi Arabia. You do the math. With American political interest seated so deeply in Saudi trade and the forthcoming war targeting Iraq and Afghanistan rather than Saudi Arabia, it didn't take long at all for people to start crying "oil!"

Eventually the burst of patriotism faded as the bullets began to fly and the war abroad became real. Almost simultaneously, disdain and distrust for government and politicians grew at an alarming rate reminiscent of the Vietnam era.

I watched my first battle on television during a high school engineering class. The screen was bright green, the aftermath of the night vision-recording device the footage was being broadcast over. The invasion of Baghdad went fairly smoothly from an American perspective. This is the battle that I remember seeing. Operation Shock and Awe proved to the world that the U.S. wasn't afraid to get its hands dirty in order to eliminate threats to our way of life. Our air forces and technology were pronounced and superior. Seeing a war televised in real time was an amazing thing to see. It was glorious, but messy. Not everything seemed to go as smoothly as it was meant to. I'm sure that some innocent Iraqi people were harmed or killed. There was collateral damage.

We all wanted to be a part of the fight, but students were generally discouraged from following their lust to join the military. It looked like an easy win, and it felt just. One Vietnam War veteran and a police officer in my borough discouraged his own son, a distinguished graduate from Valley Forge Military Academy from joining, saying that "the war would be over by the time you finish basic training."

He was wrong. The war raged on. The Global War on Terrorism would continue for more than ten more years.

A few years after 9/11 I had become an adult and a high school graduate. My best friend asked me to join the Army with him. I declined and held off because my mother and grandmother wanted me to be the first member of my family to ever earn a college degree. I reluctantly promised them that I would try to get a bachelor's degree before joining the fight. When it came time to choose a college I had a hard time, but the promise of going to a school with an ROTC program appealed to both my family's and my own wishes. I even applied to the Virginia Military Institute, but after a long talk with an officer recruiter and a visit to Thiel College, I knew that Greenville, Pennsylvania was the place for me. I fell in love with the small college and believed that to pass up the chance to wrestle at the collegiate level would be to turn my back on a different aspiration.

College was the happiest four years of my life. I loved it there. I felt truly at home. I completely reinvented myself, and allowed myself to feel accepted. I had relationships, got drunk, snorted Adderall, crammed for tests, and worked my ass off. I lost my way a couple of times, but there were always good people around me to steer me back on track. I'll always be a Thiel Tomcat. I wrestled for four years on four conference championship teams and was a frat guy, often seen wearing my Delta Sigma Phi letter shirt with cut-off sleeves.

In my junior year I realized, however, that I had a serious problem. I was tipping the scales at over 350 pounds. I was fat. I had an eating disorder. The system of losing and gaining weight that I endured to sustain the correct weight for wrestling was dangerous. On top of that, my eating habits were horrible. I knew what the right habits were, but I couldn't bring myself to actually do them. It was a horrible feeling, and my understanding of addiction and substance abuse are because of my own demons and constant battle with weight.

I had to hit rock bottom in order to crawl out of that sinkhole. A sour relationship and a call from a lieutenant saying I wasn't fit for military service engulfed me in both a sea of negativity and of motivation. I started working out every day, for over twelve hours a day. With determination and the support of my three amazing roommates and friends, I changed my eating habits and worked much harder than usual on the wrestling mats.

The work and the tears paid off. In less than one year's time I had transformed my body, losing over 156 pounds. I did it to be a soldier. Coach Thurber, the head wrestling coach, bestowed upon me the Richard Luchette Memorial Trophy despite two disappointing individual losses at the Baldwin Wallace Invitational in Ohio. I am an ultra-competitive person and I hate to lose. I wanted to exit college as an NCAA All-American. That didn't even come close to happening. So, as in many instances in my life, I walked away from what should have been a very positive experience all around, feeling that I still had something to prove, both to myself and to others. In 2007 I graduated college with a bachelor's degree in history. Time hasn't slowed down since. My college years represented the first time in my life, despite adversity, that I truly felt loved from every angle. I had not felt that way prior to Thiel College, and have rarely felt that way since.

Immediately after graduating I received news that my best friend— the same friend that had asked me to join the Army alongside him just four years earlier—had died in Iraq. I was devastated. I had made good on my promise to my mom and Grandma and graduated college, but I felt like I should have been there with him. It was time to do the deed and sign up, to put my money where my mouth was.

I enlisted in the 28TH Infantry Division of the U.S. Army and was activated for initial active duty training on my birthday of that year, 2007. Before I left, my Uncle Wally treated me to lunch. Uncle Wally wasn't actually related to me by blood, but Aunt Pin and Uncle Wally had been supportive of me since we first met. They were a pleasant consequence of one of the jobs that my grandmother worked to salvage a part of my childhood. Grandma had been a personal care assistant to Aunt Pin's mother. Aunt Pin and she became great friends and have been family to us ever since. They funded my undergraduate college education; without them I wouldn't have been able to afford a private liberal arts college, and they did more than their share to foster my military aspirations.

On this particular luncheon it was just Uncle Wally and I. I was about to embark for Fort Sill, home of the field artillery. We ate and chatted. Then he clunked down a metal object on the table. I didn't know what it was aside from it being obviously old. It was some sort of crest that looked like it came straight out of *Game of Thrones*. It was a medallion that would have been worn by Scots, by Highlanders, into battle, Uncle Wally explained. It was a family crest. The insignia included a dove or some type of game bird; a belt representing the British soldiery of the time, and the Latin phrase *sine timore*, meaning "without fear." He explained to me that war was like death, that millions of people had done it before me, and that millions would do it after me, so there was simply no reason at all to be afraid. Without fear—I chose to adopt the phrase as my own.

# THE ARMY

**I** **JOINED DURING WARTIME.** The Army needed bodies and would have taken almost anyone to meet their needs. I was colorblind which limited what I could do, my choices being initially limited to a truck driver or a human resources specialist. I chose the latter.

I was able to pass what was called the Vivid Color Vision Test. This test required me to demonstrate that I had the ability to separate a deck of cards—half green, half red—into two distinguishable piles. Passing the Vivid Color Vision Test meant that there were training opportunities available to me that would have never been an option in peacetime, just a few years prior. Careers like Airborne, Air Assault, or Ranger School could indeed be a reality for a colorblind person like me, but I had to want it bad enough.

Another hang-up threatened to derail my military aspirations. Just prior to shipping off for boot camp, the Army discovered an error in my contract: I would not be able to receive the full amount of the monetary signing bonus that I was promised. I could walk away or continue. I'll be honest—I was scared. I was having reservations. At the same time, I knew that the Army needed me, that I needed the Army, and that this was my destiny. I chose to stay the course. A few days later I was boarding a bus in Lawton, Oklahoma headed for Fort Sill for Basic Combat Training, more commonly known as boot camp. Fort Sill was Army Training and Doctrine Command's premier all-male combat arms training facility that produced the next generation of both Army and Marine Corps field artillery.

Being diagnosed as colorblind, I was not permitted to enlist into the artillery as a 13F (forward observer). I was also kept from being an infantryman, or joining the armored tank divisions, my top choices. Instead, I was presented with the option to become a human resources specialist, which I took. However, to appease my disappointment, the Army allowed me to attend basic training at Fort Sill, known for its hard-core, old-school Army training.

The bus screeched to a halt at the Fort Sill post where I and the other soldier recruits waited onboard. It wasn't until twenty minutes later that we saw a brown, round hat closing in, the infamous hat of a drill sergeant. He poked his head in and, looking at the bus driver, said, "Good afternoon sir." Then he turned to us. "Get off my fucking bus right now you pieces of shit!" Various insults continued.

As soon as we got off the bus we were put into push-up position. The barrage continued for half an hour. Then we were led into a building to process into the Fort Sill System. Just a couple of months earlier I was a drunken college frat boy with no life experience worth mentioning, and now here I was at one of the most elite Army bases in the nation. Fort Sill was new and exciting and horrifying to me all at once.

When we finished our paperwork it was almost three o'clock in the morning. We were escorted to the barracks where other soldiers were already sleeping. When the light turned on, not a soul moved in their racks. They knew not to. "Get the fuck to sleep," the Drill Sergeant screamed. "Wake-up's at 0800!" I laid down in my clothes on a mattress with no sheets and, unable to sleep, closed my eyes pretending to rest, but anxious at what would come next.

I thought I would wake up to the intense training of boot camp; instead I discovered the 95TH Reception Battalion. I was put with group Alpha Delta. There were thirteen of us, a baker's dozen, and so we came to call ourselves the Dirty Dozen, a tribute to the old war movie starring Lee Marvin.

For a solid week we slept a minimum of ten hours per night. We ate three meals a day at the best cafeteria (DEFAC) on post. We weren't permitted to exercise and, if punished, we could not be made to do more than ten push-ups. They were undoing all we had done to prepare for the Army by making us fat, weak, and sleep dependent. The days weren't completely unproductive, though. We got uniforms, haircuts, and shots. After about a week of this, the actual day came where we would be shuffled to a different area on the base to begin the real boot camp experience—the experience that Hollywood references in movies like *Full Metal Jacket* or *An Officer and a Gentleman*. It should have been obvious what was coming—the harshness of military entry training during wartime—but the comfort of the past few weeks had set in and it caught us unaware.

We were all called into formation, standing at attention in neat little rows as thirty drill sergeants hovered around us. A First Sergeant, named Easley, from Bravo Battery of the 1st Battalion 79TH Field Artillery saluted a Sergeant Gonzalez from the 95TH. In this action he effectively assumed command of our group. First Sergeant Easley was the sort of old salt that liked to make soldiers cry. Breaking people down was fun for him. He was as tough as they came. A veteran of multiple combat engagements, he stood well over six feet tall. He often had a bulge in his lower lip—chewing tobacco. This was the person that we would be encouraged to emulate in the coming weeks, a crazy, snarky, rude, tough, merciless senior enlisted soldier.

He assumed command of our group with an evil joker-esque smile on his face. He knew that he had plentiful raw material in the recruits before him. We were all just unfinished chunks of stupid lard waiting to be forged into steel. A small flag called a guidon was unfurled with our platoon lettering. "Welcome to the Bull Dogs," said the First Sergeant. There were several more seemingly random salutes, and a lot of pomp and circumstance that many of us were simply too new to understand. Then First Sergeant snapped to attention as he addressed the Sergeants that were standing off to our left side. "Drill Sergeants, take charge of your troops!"

Pure chaos followed.

There was screaming, weapons discharging into the air, and confusion all around. We were transported to our "starship" (the barracks area) on huge cattle wagons—literally, wagons used to move live beef, which is typical of military transport in Oklahoma. With no seats, everyone stood. We were not permitted to make noise of any kind. Drill Sergeant Cannon screamed as we finally arrived at the barracks, the place where we would live for the next ten weeks "Walking stops here! You pussies better fucking move your asses!" reverberated behind us as we broke into a run. The language was profane, loud, and jumbled.

We dumped all of our gear on the cement drill pad for a full showdown, dumping out anything and everything that we had onto the ground. Anything that wasn't military issue was confiscated including paper, envelopes, aspirin, pictures—you name it. We were pushed and shoved as we hurriedly made our bunks. There was a right way to make your bed. There was a right way to organize your locker. There was a right way to do everything, with only one standard to meet.

The barracks structure for the U.S. Army probably hasn't evolved much since World War I. Each soldier has a bunk in which to sleep and a wall locker to house his personal items. The locker was to be arranged according to charts. The charts were laminated pieces of white paper. They had tracings of various items on them. You could see the outline of where you would put your dress shoes, or your rolled socks, or even your rifle. Everything was mapped out so that soldiers knew exactly what the expectation was. This was an early test to see how well we could pay attention to detail. Every locker looks identical to the next, and should at all times. Inspections occur often. The area is to be kept immaculately clean (I buffed my first floor at Fort Sill.) Keeping tidy was a nearly impossible feat, considering the intensity of training. We had huge blocks of instruction in weapons, lifesaving techniques, drill and ceremony—everything that defines a professional soldier in the world's greatest army.

Our drill sergeants were all hardened combat veterans. Some of them probably suffered mental anguish and had to face the unrelenting reality of Post-Traumatic Stress Disorder as a result. Some men were great. DS Klein, DS Cannon, and DS Debourban put me in the best shape of my life, both physically and mentally. But some sergeants were not so great. Physical abuse did happen. In the "new Army", sergeants aren't allowed to strike a soldier unless on a weapons range. Unfortunately for us, all of Fort Sill was designated as an artillery weapons range at the time. I took my licks. I have no doubt that if what happened to us happened today, the instructors would be brought up on charges under the Uniformed Code of Military Justice. In an odd way that idea is disconcerting. The roughness of the training is what made it effective. The Army no longer trains soldiers by using violence or abuse as a motivator, or at least when acts like this do happen today and are discovered they are considered as crimes under the uniform code of military justice, and as conduct not becoming of a serviceman. There are different schools of thought out there as to whether or not the next generation "nicer" Army will be an effective one.

One day, after a long road march, two Marines approached us (the Marine Corps also utilized Fort Sill for all of their artillery training needs). They looked at us and exclaimed that we had it way worse than they had had at Paris Island. The words shocked us. A Marine had just admitted to a group of Army basic training soldiers that basic training was harder than Marine boot camp. Such a statement should never be made between rivalry branches. It was right at that moment we knew how bad we had it.

Training sucked. In ways we were lucky though. We got to throw live grenades, feeling the percussion shatter through our bones. The Marines didn't have that luxury. We also got to interact with Iraqi nationals during training, not actors dressed up in costumes. All the extras brought a certain realism to what we were doing. It would be no surprise that within a year of graduation most of us would find ourselves in the harsh terrains of Iraq or Afghanistan. We were preparing for war and learning accountability through hardship.

I had only one personal issue throughout my basic training experience and it was an embarrassing one. Treadwell Tower was a forty-foot high fortress built to teach rappelling skills and instill confidence. I completed the obstacles within the tower: a one rope bridge, two rope bridge, forty foot ladder, rappel wall, and rope swing. When I finished, I was out of water and exhausted from the obstacles, as well as the forced march with fifty-pound ruck sacks that we had undertaken to get there. Standing atop the forty-foot tower I began to feel dizzy. I went to a drill sergeant from another platoon to make my case. "Drill Sergeant, I'm out of water and I need a break." I was met with a curt reply. "Fuck off. You can rest when you get your ass down my cargo net." I moved to the point where the cargo net dropped off the forty-foot tower. I put one foot on the rope and then the lights went out.

I fell forty feet and landed on my head between two large gymnastics mats. Apparently, I got right up and walked around, but I don't remember any of that. At the hospital, the doctors were distraught that my neck and spine had not been stabilized before I was moved, and that I arrived in a Humvee rather than in an ambulance almost four hours after the fall. I don't know what happened in those hours. Everyone told me that I should have died.

Sitting in a hospital bed I had to force myself to urinate to save myself from having a catheter inserted.

A nurse gave me a phone number, telling me that the sergeants from my unit had called and asked if they could punish me for falling. The nurse told me to call her if they tried it.

When I got back to the barracks, my platoon was concerned for my well-being, but to the rest of the battery I was a laughing stock and the butt of many a joke. I wasn't permitted to call home or see a chaplain. My good friend, Ken Ramsay, woke me up every half an hour as prescribed by the doctors. Ramsay also had to re-teach me how to tie my boots. The memory of that simple task was completely wiped out. I have no idea what else I lost.

Ramsay was also colorblind, and a Nebraska National Guardsman who would be with me throughout my entire initial training journey. Eventually, he would come to invite me to be the best man in his wedding, which sadly I was not able to attend because of the deployments that would come.

For a few weeks after the fall, life was very hard. I couldn't bend over or twist without experiencing intense pain and I was anticipating my punishment. It never came. Perhaps they figured that the pain was enough.

A tragic event happened a few weeks later and led to an enhancement of safety protocols throughout the post. A young private by the name of Danny Fisher from the 1ST Battalion 40TH Field Artillery was shot and killed by a fifty-caliber machine gun round. It was a horrible accident that many of us felt the Army attempted to cover up and minimize. It showed us all that the risk was very real.

Afterwards, things started to change at Fort Sill. We spent hours painting dummy rounds with blue spray paint, a safety consideration that had previously been neglected. We also attended our first class on muzzle awareness. Many of the recruits were hunters and woodsman, and could point out things that our leaders did wrong from a basic safety perspective.

I did my share of work details. I raked dirt. I guarded empty bleachers. I got "smoked"—our term for corrective action, requiring more pushups than I imagine any ROTC cadet ever did.

Fall came and went and graduation was upon us before we knew it. We all looked magnificent in our green uniforms with their golden buttons and silver marksmanship badges. It was an accomplishment to have made it to the end, and my grandmother made the trip all the way from Pittsburgh to see me graduate. But on my day off-base with Grandma I was unable to relax. I was paranoid and shell shocked from everything I had recently been through and I'm sure I didn't act like myself. I was indoctrinated properly into a world of blood and killing. In my heart, though, I knew that I had made it. I was a soldier. We were all soldiers. We were one step closer to doing the job that we all signed up to do.

# RANK AND FILE

IN TRYING TO UNDERSTAND the Army, it helps to understand rank. Everyone has a rank and that rank is associated to a pay grade (how much money you can make). There are many variables such as time in service, number of dependents, and which benefits a soldier selects which determine the total take home pay amount. In 2009 an Army Private (E-1) with four months or more of active duty time would net $1,399.50 per month, or an annual salary of only $16,794 according to www.militaryrates.com. When deployed to a combat zone there was other monetary incentives like hazardous duty pay and tax free earnings, but generally the vast majority of soldiers that I served with were not paid well, especially considering the inherent danger and required time commitment of being deployed. Here is a run down of rank in the army and how it works.

| CATEGORY | Insignia of the United States Army | | | | | | |
|---|---|---|---|---|---|---|---|
| | E-1 | E-2 | E-3 | E-4 | | E-5 | E-6 |
| **ENLISTED** (Green and Gold) | no insignia Private | Private | Private 1st Class | Corporal | Specialist | Sergeant | Staff Sergeant |
| | E-7 | E-8 | | E-9 | | | |
| | Sergeant 1st Class | Master Sergeant | 1st Sergeant | Sergeant Major | Command Sergeant Major | Sergeant Major of the Army | |
| | W-1 | W-2 | W-3 | W-4 | | W-5 | |
| **WARRANT OFFICER** (Silver and Black) | Warrant Officer | Chief Warrant Officer | Chief Warrant Officer | Chief Warrant Officer | | Master Warrant Officer | |
| | 0-1 | 0-2 | 0-3 | 0-4 | 0-5 | 0-6 | |
| **COMPANY AND FIELD GRADE OFFICER** (Gold and Silver) | (gold) 2nd Lieutenant | (silver) 1st Lieutenant | (silver) Captain | (gold) Major | (silver) Lieutenant Colonel | (silver) Colonel | |
| | 0-7 | 0-8 | 0-9 | 0-10 | | 0-11 | |
| **GENERAL OFFICER** (Silver) | Brigadier General | Major General | Lieutenant General | General | | General of the Army | |

*Figure 1. A listing of U.S. Army ranks with insignia.*

## ENLISTED

If you joined the Army right out of high school you would typically enlist as a Private (Pay grade E-1). E-1 Privates do not wear any rank on their sleeves. They are the lowest of the low. When it comes time to do undesirable task these would be the first soldiers to be called upon. E-1 Privates become E-2 Privates. These are Privates with one stripe on their sleeve. Generally all E-1 and E-2 Privates are lumped together by their leaders—all are simply called "Private".

Next comes Private First Class (E-3 pay grade), also known as "PFC". PFCs are typically viewed as eager to prove themselves and good team members.

Then comes the E-4 Pay Grade. Both the rank of Specialist and Corporal fall under this pay grade. Both can act as Army team leaders. Corporals have been selected for special leadership opportunities. Specialists are considered enlisted men, whereas Corporals represent the first rank that is considered to be a Non-Commissioned Officer (NCO).

## NCOs

NCOs are often recognized as the backbone of the Army. Sergeants, Staff Sergeants, Sergeants First Class, Master Sergeants, First Sergeants, Sergeant Majors and Command Sergeant Majors are all members of the NCO Corps. The various categories of Sergeant Majors represent the senior-most men that enlisted in the Army. Often times Sergeant Majors have over twenty years of service. All ranks Sergeant First Class (E-7) and above are validated by the U.S. Congress.

## WARRANT OFFICERS

Warrant officers are men and women with a high level of skill in their occupation. They are not technically enlisted, nor are they NCOs or commissioned officers. Warrant officers are addressed as "Mister", not "Sir". Enlisted men and NCOs will both salute a warrant officer. The majority of helicopter pilots in the Army are Warrant Officers. Warrants typically are very dependable and knowledgeable. They are fairly rare when compared to the other categories of ranks in the Army.

## COMMISSIONED OFFICERS

Commissioned Officers are the management and planning class of the Army. There are many pathways to become a commissioned officer. All officers are college graduates. Attending a university Reserve Officer Training Course (ROTC), Graduating from Officer Candidate School (OCS), graduating from a federal service academy, receiving a direct appointment (most common in lawyers, physicians, and religious fields), or in rare cases receiving a battlefield commission (promoted due to excellence in combat) are the established ways to become an officer. Army commissioned officers include Second Lieutenants, First Lieutenants, Captains, Majors, Lieutenant Colonels, Colonels, Brigadier Generals, Major Generals, Lieutenant Generals, and Generals, which all make up the officer corps. The pay grades for officers are O-1 to O-9, respectively.

The U.S. Army is largely organized based on the European military tradition. Understanding the structural composition of the Army can make reading about American military operations both simpler and more enjoyable. By the time soldiers complete their Basic Combat

Training (boot camp), they are all aware of how the military is organized and have learned where they fit into the established hierarchy. There can be anywhere between 8 and 24 soldiers in a squad. In most cases two squads will make up a section. I was part of the S-1 section, which admittedly had fewer members than would be typical for serving an organization the size of our infantry regiment. Two or more squads (typically 4) are categorized as a platoon, and multiple platoons make up a company. Companies are identified using the phonetic alphabet (Alpha Company, Bravo, Charlie, etc.) In some cases company leadership will substitute the phonetic for something more unique. Alpha Company can be called "Animal" Company, or "Anarchy" Company. Battalions also regularly have a headquarters element company, which is identified as Headquarters and Headquarters Company (HHC). A company typically has 100 to 200 soldiers, and a battalion is a combat unit of 500 to 800 soldiers, composed of multiple companies. My battalion was the 1st Battalion of the 112TH Infantry Regiment. Three to five battalions, approximately 1,500 to 4,000 soldiers, comprise a brigade. My battalion was part of the 56TH Stryker Brigade. Multiple brigades make up a division. The 56TH Stryker Brigade was part of the 28TH Infantry Division, popularly known as the "Bloody Bucket". Multiple divisions comprise the U.S. Army as a whole.

# GOODBYE FORT SILL

THE FOLLOWING DAY RAMSAY and I sat next to each other on an airplane heading for Fort Jackson, South Carolina. We were told that Advanced Individual Training (AIT) would be much more relaxed than Basic Combat Training. That was an understatement to say the least. We made our way to Echo Company of the 369TH AG Battalion. Echo was next to the Army's Drill Sergeant School, but its proximity held no bearing on the structure or intensity of our training. Everywhere we moved we seemed to be in a disorderly gaggle: people talked in formation and were undisciplined. To graduates from Fort Sill (like me) or Fort Benning, the Fort Jackson soldiers were a complete and utter joke, a menace to the force, and a disgrace to the uniform. They didn't respect authority because I don't think that they were ever made to as we were. I believe that this is why so many in other branches look down on the average Army soldier. A person who goes to McDonald's in Pittsburgh will get the same Big Mac as they would in Los Angeles. Such is not the case with soldiering. What I refer to as the "Fort Jackson Soldiers" could have just as easily went to Boot Camp at Benning, Sill, or Knox, but they didn't.

They either won or lost that lottery depending on your perspective. As a result they tested a new sort of training in which soldiers were asked to gauge their own stress levels, given cards to hand to their drill sergeants when things got stressful so that they could have a ten-minute reprieve. They were permitted to use their cell phones during certain portions of their training. They were soldiers just like me, but had received the new age training rather than the old school training. The differences were noticeable. Soldiers brought up in the artillery or infantry are different than soldiers brought up in support. I'm not saying better, just different. The combat arms soldiers of the past were being phased out for these new entitled, trophy-generation warriors. My squad was the last major group trained under the old standard. Perhaps we were obsolete; who am I to say?

I wished with all of my heart that I was an infantryman. If I was an infantryman I never would have been subjected to the relaxed conditions that existed at Fort Jackson. My faith in what the military was and vision of what it should have been would have been protected, for at least a while longer. I wasn't there to have fun or see the world or get a new career. I was there because I wanted to fight, and I was bloodthirsty. I often tried to perform at a higher level, putting in extra effort outside of the regular training day, to ensure that no matter where I went in the military I would be able to conform to the highest standards. There were many soldiers, both old and new, who felt that the changes made in the Armed Forces in order to meet the demands of the Global War on Terrorism hurt the long term national defense capabilities of the United States. My experience at Fort Jackson highlighted many of these frowned-upon changes.

The military transformed to meet the challenges associated with the insurgency, which appeared after the initial invasion of Iraq. In doing so, it unknowingly threatened its own appearance to the world as a military superpower and shook our empire worldwide. The war effort and the economy had a mutual effect on one another. Fuel prices sky-rocketed as a result, and the value of the dollar dropped while people in our own country struggled. Political analysts on both sides of the aisle argued over ideas but never offered executable solutions. Public perception of the military changed, too. There were many who disliked the military. Everybody was a critic. Few of those with commentary cared enough to pick up a rifle and join the fight.

The War on Terror has been compared to the Vietnam Conflict; it was the most unpopular military action of my lifetime. Being a soldier in today's Army got me a few thank you handshakes but many more scoffs and people talking behind my back.

Since, as human resources soldiers, our primary duty was to take care of combat arms soldiers, we called ourselves the "Chairborne Rangers". In training we spent much of our time behind computer screens, filling out forms. Combat patches were hard to find at the Adjutant General Corps School compared to Fort Sill. Not many people seemed to have been deployed before. Maybe it was better that way.

My instructors had done their time, however. Staff Sergeant Wheeless was a good guy that had been deployed with the 1st Armored Division. Sergeant Peters earned the Bronze Star for Valor and the Purple Heart for his service with the 1st Cavalry Division. I was in the company of heroes. Our platoon grew close very fast. We ate together and when off post we partied together. It wasn't uncommon for males and females to sneak off into the woods together. Males and females living and working together presented an entirely different military than what I saw at Fort Sill during basic training, and that was just the start.

Physical training was easier and foul language was checked at the door. The excessive profanity we had picked during basic training was now prohibited. I scraped through AIT as an honor graduate. At the end of AIT I was awarded the MOS classification of 42A10, which means that the Army certified me of being capable of doing my job with little or no supervision. It meant that I had what it took. From that point onward, I was a fully qualified soldier. I would graduate from some of the military's toughest school's to prepare me for the realities of a modern army at war.

# HOME FOR A REST

**F**OLLOWING AIT, I WENT back to my home in Pittsburgh and joined my regular unit, the 128TH Forward Support Battalion. It was a coed unit with a laid back demeanor. Within 15 minutes of my arrival though, SSG Roman corrected me for standing at parade rest while speaking to her. This is historically how junior enlisted soldiers show respect to non-commissioned officers. This signaled a huge change for me. Training was over. I was now part of the regular force. The regular force was much nicer, friendlier, and relaxed than what Training and Doctrine Command had prepared me for. These were regular people working regular jobs that didn't feel the need to follow every word of military courtesy to the letter, at least at this unit. Many suggested that the 128TH was a final destination for long-time soldiers whose military careers had gone stagnant. This was unfortunate, and something that future battalion commanders there would work hard to remedy.

I made friends quickly and grew to respect each person's qualities. Despite the camaraderie, I was disappointed that I was not in an infantry unit. I was not the point of the spear. I wondered if I would ever have the chance to prove myself in combat. If my unit deployed, I knew it would be to Germany, Kosovo, or Kuwait—all places relatively calm compared to Iraq. I didn't want that. I wanted to fight.

Believing that I would not go to war soon, I made plans to go to Officer Candidate School (OCS). I had been contractually guaranteed an OCS slot at enlistment. I finished college so I felt I deserved to be an officer. That would have been the typical track for a person in my situation to follow. Officers oversee the management and planning aspects of missions, while often times NCOs carry out those orders. Both are types of leaders, but both exercise different types of leadership. Lieutenant Subulsky was in charge of officer strength for our region. He convinced me that since I was going to get my graduate degree, ROTC might be the best option. ROTC meant I could go to school for free and work toward a commission as a U.S. Army officer. In addition, I would be non-deployable. I wanted to be an infantry officer, and after waiting for so long I thought ROTC would finally give me my chance. A week later, I met with Major Morris at the University of Pittsburgh and filled out the preliminary forms to become a cadet via a cross-town affiliation program with Duquesne University, where I enrolled in graduate school. I was on the way to becoming a Lieutenant.

My military career is unique compared to most in that during my time in the armed forces I was an enlisted soldier, an SMP Cadet (officer candidate) for less than a month, and an NCO (corporal) for less than two weeks. An SMP Cadet and an enlisted soldier are two separate positions, but have major overlaps. SMP cadets continue their enlisted duties but also take on additional officer training opportunities, usually at a local college and are paid at the rate of E-5 which is typically a higher pay rate than they would warrant as a lower enlisted soldier. I spent very little time in ROTC, but was proud to participate on their Ranger Challenge Team before getting the call to deploy. Because ROTC Cadets are not deployable the choice was mine. Would I drop out of the cadetship, resume my enlisted duties and go to war—learning by doing, or would I maintain my cadetship, stay home, and continue my march towards an officers commission by learning what I could from the officers appointed over me? It was a tough call.

# MOBILIZATION

**M**Y UNIT'S WARNING ORDER for Kuwaiti service had been bumped back several times, from October 2009 to 2010 and eventually 2011. The reality of combat seemed a far off possibility. So, I had made all due preparations to begin my master's degree at Duquesne University in August 2008 as the recipient of an ROTC scholarship. At the time I excelled in the Army Physical Fitness Test and was an expert marksman. Everything was going my way.

I still couldn't shake my desire to be deployed and I knew that my time would come after graduate school as an officer. But on August 13TH I received a misleading phone call stating that there were no SMP "slots" available in my battalion for cadets or officer candidates. It wasn't until later that I found out this statement was entirely false. It was an attempt to protect the battalions' many non-deployable, retirement-age soldiers by making new cadets deployable as specialists. This didn't just happen in my unit, but in battalions all throughout the state of Pennsylvania. Cadets would deploy—they just wouldn't carry the title of cadet, but of Private or Private First Class. This hadn't happened in U.S. military history since the Virginia Military Institute cadets marched off to fight the Yankees during the American Civil War. The move was a part of a series of small unit politics, which directly violated U.S. Army regulations.

The 56TH Stryker Brigade out of Fort Indiantown Gap was heading to Iraq. They needed people in my military occupation specialty, or MOS. In honesty I did get deployed under misleading circumstances and with incorrect information. Many other soldiers did as well. But ultimately, I had wanted to join the efforts overseas for sometime. On September 19TH I began my first deployment as an American soldier. I dropped out of school and prepared for the inevitable tour of duty. The needs of the Army outweighed the contractual obligations, which the Army had made to me. Despite obvious contractual violations and the manipulative way in which many young men and women were forced to join the deployment, I was ready and anxious to prove my worth.

In August of that year I worked at the armory. I had to make certain that I received all the equipment I would need for the deployment. Most of the equipment had been on order for months. I got my orders to SRP, a complete series of medical, mental, and administrative assignments. It meant a four-day weekend at Fort Indiantown Gap in Central Pennsylvania. Soldiers had to pass each station at SRP in order to receive appropriate medical clearance to deploy overseas in a combat capacity. I let my professors, academic advisor, and ROTC instructor know that I had been called to deploy. I was sure that my situation wasn't unique. I met with a notary public and filled out a rental agreement for my mobilization folder so that I could be compensated by the government for storing my belongings while I was gone. I had a lot to do to wrap things up at home and little time to do it. While I was preparing to leave, I learned from Captain Heiple that I would have become the Platoon Sergeant for my ROTC platoon. Regrettably, I couldn't accept the position; I left early the next morning for four days at Fort Indiantown Gap.

Details of the deployment leaked out slowly, but nothing came directly from the Army. We learned from the media that we would be deployed to the pseudo-remote area of Iraq—Al Taji—where we would relieve other soldiers. We were to be only a small part of the massive force.

I spent the next four days at Fort Indiantown Gap going through the SRP process. After the weekend I would know whether or not I would actually be deployed. There was an unhealthy lack of concrete information. It's important to take a moment here to clear up the tension and explain my uncertainty towards the deployment. I had been told that I was deploying to Iraq and I had been training to accomplish that goal, however many soldiers had been told the same thing in the past only to have their deployments cancelled, or postponed, or to become re-categorized as humanitarian missions on friendlier ground. Despite all of my efforts to figure things out, and the personal actions that I took to accommodate the deployment, going to Iraq wouldn't be a certainty until I was actually physically on the airplane en route to Kuwait. Part of this lack of knowledge may have been intentional as the less we all knew, the less we could talk about on Facebook or other social media, and the less the enemy could figure out in advance. Honestly though, the truth is that the armed forces can be an extremely unorganized beast at times. There is logistically a lot of things that go into moving large numbers of troops around. So what can a soldier do until he knows what is actually happening? There was only one thing. All you could do was wait.

August 25, 2008. It was a Monday. I have always hated Mondays because they always seemed to signal an end to the carefree weekend. I'd just gotten home from a four-day weekend at the Gap and was reflecting on the events that had transpired. When we got to the Gap, it felt like we were back in initial entry training all over again. The first day we had formations all the time, mostly for accountability. We were yelled at by a Master Sergeant Gunnel who screamed at us like basic trainees, claiming that if "3,000 Gooks" couldn't kill him in Vietnam then there was no way soldiers like us could. Some people laughed at the Sergeant's rough demeanor. It was old school. We also went through medical processing and got our shots, physical exam, eye exam, hearing test, and dental exam. Largely it was a lot of confusion, yelling, and waiting in lines.

The second day we did administrative processing and took care of our pay issues, life insurance, and identification—basically everything that makes sure that our pay is directed in the way we want during the deployment. "Hurry up and wait," was the central theme of the day. In some cases we were only given time to eat once a day, violating active duty Army's only promise of "three squares a day."

The third day was equipment issue. Everything was top of the line Army Combat Uniform (ACU) digital camouflage pattern. We got full-blown assault vests, assault packs, extra-large framed rucksacks, combat first aid kits, IBA body armor, the new lightweight Army combat helmets (ACH), new desert boots, and more. No expense was spared to outfit us.

The final day was a recovery day. I met a Private from McKeesport who, like me, was an ROTC cadet. He did not want to go to war. The Sergeant Major at SRP told him that he wasn't deployable because he was a valid ROTC student. I had all my ROTC paperwork in but had been told that there was nothing that could be done for me. Cadets couldn't deploy. He was there due to the same mistake that I was there, except where he had fought the idea I had generally embraced it. He got out of going to Iraq. He would return instead to a college classroom. I contemplated contacting the post's Inspector General (IG) and making this a bigger issue. That's when I realized that the Private was complaining because he was afraid. As an SMP Cadet, I too was eventually given a chance to "get out" of deployment, as were several others. Many took the deal. It was too late to return to graduate school for me by this point. I would at least miss a semester. The opportunity to go home with my tail tucked between my legs under the pretense that doing so would somehow make me a better military leader than an actual combat tour of duty could was an offer I had to decline for both my feelings of patriotism and realities of time and finance that had already been imposed upon by these events. I was locked in.

Yet the American troops over there desperately needed help, and they needed to be relieved. I had to help my brothers. This deployment meant gaining experience that would benefit me when I resumed my goal of officership upon my return. I accepted the challenge and opportunity for martial honor. Service in the Middle East was no joke and I didn't look at it as one. I'd already lost friends in this war. I confirmed my commitment to be deployed on the last day of training. I knew how to stand up and be a leader. No more talking, it was time to walk the walk. It was go time!

# BUSY AS HELL

O N THE BUS RIDE back to Pittsburgh from the base I had a million thoughts running around in my head. There was so much to do in so very little time. I had to move out of my apartment, find storage for my furniture, and finalize leaving graduate school in a manner that facilitated an eventual return to academic study.

On August 28TH, Sergeant McDine, my readiness NCO, gave me orders to attend Operation Atlas in Fort Indiantown Gap. I was going back. This two-week block of instruction marked my second annual training event. This training served as pre-deployment training in order to familiarize those soldiers who did not attend annual training with the 56TH Stryker Brigade. It served as Stryker (armored troop transport) orientation with weapons qualifications for the rifle, pistol, squad automatic weapon, and fifty caliber machine-gun. I expected it to be more difficult than the training I attended earlier in the summer at Fort Pickett, Virginia. I also expected it to be more orientated towards mechanized infantry. While it failed to meet many of my high expectations, it was, in retrospect, worthwhile training.

# WE SHALL FIGHT IN THE SHADE

**T**HE TRAINING AT OPERATION Atlas was a considered by many to be a great success. The training was more long term than other similar training events. It went on for weeks. We trained by repetition. It felt like we did everything 1000 times. I'd spent several days in marksmanship training, several more in vehicle training, more on movement and obstacle courses. As with all Army training I cleaned a lot as well. I mopped and buffed floors, wiped windows, and collected garbage for the dumpsters. When we arrived at Operation Atlas it was a warm, early summer day. The sky was filled with transparent clouds. As the first day went on, I became a member of Hotel Company. My platoon sergeant was an excellent non-commissioned officer, one of the few left in the Army that could wear the jungle warfare combat patch for service in Panama. My squad leader cared more about the welfare of the soldiers under his control than anyone I have ever met. It is a wonder that he never became an officer.

Every day was filled with training, waiting, bitching. We were a ragtag group of soldiers thrown together from all corners of the state to help meet the personnel shortages within the 56TH Stryker Brigade. I wanted to go home almost as badly as I want to prove myself as a soldier—almost. When the sun was too hot, we would take our poncho liners, construct a makeshift shelter, and nap in the shade in a manner that would make any Special Operations soldier proud.

# THE NEW GUY

SEPTEMBER 19, 2008: The training, shots, and hardship of SRP and Atlas fading into memory, I kissed my mother and grandmother, hugged my brother, and said goodbye to friends and family.

I arrived at the Pittsburgh armory early in the morning for transport to Cambridge Springs, a small town about a half an hour away from Erie. It was the nicest armory I had ever seen in a National Guard unit: a brand new building across the street from a women's detention facility. The armory bore strong resemblance to a high school. We offloaded the buses and made our way inside to find a massive drill floor, fitness room, cafeteria, and oversized restrooms, all features unknown by Second Brigade Soldiers like me at the time. It was the Hilton of National Guard Headquarters.

My new section sergeants were resident experts of what is known in the military as the S-1 shop. The S-1 shop is the human resources wing of a battalion. Sergeant Minnick was the only one in the section with a combat patch. As an air assault veteran of the Second Infantry Division, I thought his experience would be an asset for our deployment. Those who were "backfills," or replacement warriors like me, could no longer say we were part of a different brigade. We were now part of something new, perhaps something experimental. That was the First Battalion, 112TH Infantry Stryker Brigade Combat Team's "Task Force Strong". Our Task Force was named after Strong Vincent, a hero of the American Civil War. Our unit traced its combat lineage to include Vincent, who fell at the Round Tops in Gettysburg. It was a part of the only reserve component Stryker brigade in the world.

The next several days we spent packing, marking bags, meeting people and signing out new weapons. We slept at the Edinboro Inn, a dilapidated hotel on a subpar golf course in the town of Edinboro, collegiate home of many wrestling legends. The next stop was Camp Shelby, Mississippi.

Most of the leadership of our battalion at Camp Shelby had expert infantry qualifications or Ranger training. Many had already seen combat action. With the changing political climate in the country, as well as a perceived increase of tensions in Afghanistan and occupational police action status of Iraq, I don't think anyone could know or even guess what we were about to get ourselves into. I know I didn't.

# JOINT READINESS TRAINING CENTER

**SEPTEMBER 26, 2008:** I never thought I could experience such a flight in a post-September 11TH world. We rode in coach buses directly through a checkpoint onto a dark airport runway in Erie, Pennsylvania, rifles in hand. We shook hands with three generals and the retiring Division Sergeant Major and boarded our commercial air flight. I was carrying an M4 assault rifle, a Gerber multi-tool, and a Winchester folding knife. We didn't go through any security. Soldiers with pistols littered the seats. I suppose I should feel honored to have been bestowed such trust from the airlines. Then again, if it weren't for constant federal government bailouts most of these airlines probably wouldn't have existed at that point in the first place. The government and the economy now seemed to be irrevocably intertwined. We could tell that a lot of our gear was the result of new government contracts. We were the first soldiers to be issued gear made by Under Armor. We had Converse combat boots, Oakley ballistic sunglasses. We were soldiers, but it sometimes felt like we were sponsored athletes as well. Combat had become commercialized. Many American airlines were on life support and the war effort kept many within the aviation industry employed.

The flight attendants gave us a small breakfast. It was the first flight I've ever been on that had an all-male flight attendant crew. I know that some of us would have appreciated female flight attendants; as an infantry regiment, our ranks were mostly male. Even still, the plane ride was far from comfortable. The First Sergeant, an airborne pathfinder, also new to the unit, told us that we would all be taking a urine test for drugs and alcohol as soon as we de-planed in Mississippi. He recommended that nobody use the latrine onboard the aircraft. Recommended translated to "pee and you will be punished".

Being tossed into a new group, coupled with the lingering thoughts of a deteriorating relationship with my girlfriend at the time and worries about my increasing weight and physical training quickly added to the overall stress that comes with being mobilized for war. A few nights later, one of my best friends, Marc Berry, called to tell me his grandmother had passed away. Her passing contributed to the stress and sadness, but I grew sadder still when I thought about the health issues in my own family. I was depressed, and with my stress level so high, I didn't know that I could deal with a family member passing away at that point in my life. Terrible thoughts filled my head. I knew that millions of men had gone before me to fight the wars of yesteryear with worries of their own and that millions would come after me, but still it made my heart sad.

There was plenty of joking around. In an all-male unit, Alaska Governor Palin who was running on the presidential election ticket looked better and better as the mobilization process continued. We were mentally the equivalent of a junior high football team in the locker room after a winning game. One sergeant actually sent out a mass email over the Army e-mail system (AKO). It read as follows:

*Warning: if you receive an email claiming under the subject area to contain erotic photographs of Vice Presidential Nominee Palin do not open it—it may contain a potentially devastating computer virus.*

*If you receive an email claiming under the subject area to contain erotic photographs of Hillary Clinton do not open it— it may contain erotic photographs of Hillary Clinton!*

Left and right soldiers were getting sent home. Many couldn't pass the medical screening portion of SRP. Others were injured. Sergeant Monfordini, who had been to war before, said it was better for those people to go home now. "If they don't want to be here then you don't want them by your side when bullets are flying overhead." No one really had to be there, it was true. There were so many cowards. If I was dead set on going home I could have done so right then but what would that prove? Could I live with myself if I didn't deploy with these guys? I was poised to do something great, to be a support soldier attached to a line infantry Stryker unit. Someone once said, "A man often meets his destiny on the road he took to avoid it." This was what I had asked for. I was falling in love with the infantry.

I qualified with the M4 rifle at Camp Shelby, hitting 36 out of 40 targets on the range, thanks to the new CCO red-dot integrated targeting system. I also hit 19 out of 20 targets while wearing an NBC gas mask and got passing marks on the night familiarization fire. I had struggled with the rifle early on in my career but I became an expert marksman, earning the Bronze Excellence In Competition (EIC) badge for proficiency with the M16 rifle. I was shooting more and more and loving it. Shooting relaxed me, and I eventually earned Squad Designated Marksman status.

My unit sent about a third of the battalion from Camp Shelby ahead to Fort Polk to establish our mission at the base in preparation for our Joint Readiness Training Center, better known as theatre immersion training. This increased my workload during the mobilization for about nine days. The added responsibility was welcome, but the extra stress was not.

Physical training had declined to the point where I could only work out once or twice a week. I hated that. I wanted to work out. I needed to work out. I wasn't eating right and I knew I was gaining weight. The Army Physical Fitness Test (APFT), which consisted of a timed, two-mile run, two minutes of push-ups, and two minutes of sit-ups, scared me to death. I didn't think I could pass but somehow I pulled it off. Even if I passed with a perfect score I didn't look like a soldier. I didn't want to get flagged. Flagging would suspend all pending awards and promotions, per Army regulations. I wanted to use this deployment to shed weight and come home in pristine condition. I hoped it would be possible. I had worked damn hard to lose 150 pounds to join the Army and I couldn't let that become undone because of the Army itself.

I tried to change my schedule to accommodate workouts and meals but I struggled. By Army standards I was overweight. I was reminded of it often when I looked at my infantry counterparts in the regiment. I was as well-suited to do my job as they were to do theirs. Yet I had to master elements of their job in order to call myself a soldier where many of them lacked the mental capacity, but not the heart, to do mine. It would have been easier to get into shape if I was out there on a daily basis walking on foot patrols with heavy equipment. I actually wanted to do those light infantry tasks that most soldiers complained about, but I had to spend a good part of each day behind a computer screen. The demands of my job were multi-faceted. Being physically fit is a part of being a soldier. I had begged for time to exercise; no one would care or needed to know that I had overcome an eating disorder to arrive here, or that before boot camp I had ran eight miles a day and spent 6 days a week with free weights to meet the standard to get in. Within my Tactical Operations Center (TOC) there were two captains and a major who could be called "stout." One of the majors often spoke poorly of his own stepson, a 240-pound specialist who did his job better than anyone else in the regiment possibly could have. Despite his skill, it was his size that was remarked upon. It wouldn't have taken much for that major to free up some time everyday so that our unit could do some additional physical fitness training, even on a voluntary basis. I think he didn't allow us time to work out because he didn't want to have to show up on the PT field himself. A high physical standard should be universal, regardless of how long you've been around.

The next few weeks at Fort Polk were dedicated to a field exercise, where we'd be sleeping in tents and taking part in mock missions and scenarios. There was a deep hatred growing within the brigade for our First Army Division graders, the ones who rated how we were doing, because we were more competent and better equipped as a force than they were. The soldier/graders that worked for First Army were largely National Guardsmen and Reservist who had recently completed an overseas deployment. Many of them were unemployed in their civilian careers and pursued the instructor position as a desperate effort to extend their active duty time and earn a bit of extra cash. Though all of them had indeed deployed, only a hand full of them had actually experienced combat, with maybe one or two having taken direct fire. This meant that many of my regiment's leadership had more combat experience and better training than the people who were tasked with rating our abilities. This caused an uncomfortable relationship with the First Army Division, who in fairness were doing their best to prepare us for Iraq. Our Stryker vehicles were magnificent. We were the only reserve component Stryker group in existence and one of only six Stryker brigades worldwide. These vehicles were as impervious as modern technology allowed for an infantry vehicle.

Many men made a modular uniform change of their own accord. Uniform tabs identify special skills or troops within the armed forces. Some of the more commonly known tabs are Ranger, Special Forces, Mountain, Airborne, or Sapper. These small cloth patches are placed above unit insignia to distinguish those soldiers from others. There was a push from brigade soldiers for a new subdued uniform tab reading 'Stryker' that would have recognized soldiers completing a deployment as a member of a Stryker Brigade Combat Team. It would also acknowledge the extra hours of training that went into being a Stryker crewman.

As the only National Guard Stryker Brigade in the world, there were some very special connotations associated with the tab. Our soldiers often had to leave their successful civilian jobs, places of education, and families to complete this training—training which redefined the initial reserve component enlistment contract. If officially approved, it would be the first designation of its kind. Many in my battalion wore an unofficial version of the patch, myself included, though it was often hidden under the collar.

My relationship status was confusing. Every time I talked to my girlfriend we would fight. I tried not to let it bother me, but of course it did. I couldn't help but think about the other girls that I could be with, but I was faithful to the girl I was with. Lately I'd been given a lot of extra attention from women. Going to war was like love potion no. 9. I was viewed as desirable because I was so unattainable: I was leaving the country for a year. I wasn't actively seeking a new girlfriend but I was unhappy with the one I was with. I knew I didn't have time and that it would be unfair to start something new with someone else. I just hoped that when I got back there would be someone special for me to have something real with. I was still young but I had hopes and dreams. I thought about marriage and kids and all of the things that come with growing up. Right then, I couldn't see that far into my future to predict such things. I didn't want to be alone but I had to be when preparing for life in the Army. A dream told me that I'd meet a girl that likes music and animals—someone with a great laugh, but I never had much faith in dreams. I knew I had a job to do, and hoped that when the time came my mind could be clear enough to do it.

# MY BAND OF
# BROTHERS

**E**VERY GREAT STORY has a diverse and unique set of characters. Mine is no different. People were coming in and out of my life constantly; I met so many people, many of which left as fast as they came. As I said earlier, one of my sergeants was released from the active duty Army; the one from the Second Infantry Division who I had thought was so impressive. We all expected him back sometime within the month. He never returned to us.

Then another soldier, a human resource specialist and a fueler from a support battalion, and friend left us. He was a stand-up guy, a veteran of the Kosovo campaign (KFOR). This would be his first opportunity to wear a combat patch. His support battalion, like mine, also received orders to deploy but to Camp Liberty rather than Camp Taji. He still wanted to, and would, go to Iraq, but he didn't want to do it with an Infantry regiment. The idea of the infantry was scary to many. Infantry was synonymous with front lines. On one hand, he'd be immersed in a much more lax environment, one without combat arms and one with plenty of female soldiers. On the other hand, he would probably never see a Stryker again outside of filling them with diesel. He wouldn't be going on infantry missions, and his view of combat would probably be different compared to that of a line unit like the 1-112TH. I wished he was staying with us and I think he secretly wished the same. Part of being a soldier is putting the skills taught to you to the test. The only way to do that is either in a combat zone or at times of regional emergency. At least he was still going. There were many soldiers that chose not to go at all, or shifted their unit affiliation to make life down range easier. People who wanted to play it safe sought out the aviation and support battalions whereas those that wanted to fight stayed in the infantry, cavalry, or artillery, or at least that was my perception.

All of the characters of my story come from all walks of life. Some have college degrees and some have GEDs. Some have prior service experience and some have never been outside of their one unit. These are the people who were the most important to me. Despite the differences, they are all soldiers. As soldiers, we share in a unique bond. In war, there is no hiding who you are; the truth comes out when the bullets fly. Throughout my deployment I came to depend on each one of them and they depended on me. These are the men who were with me in Iraq. We were the S-1 section, keepers of both the pen and the sword, a rag tag group of heathens who were eager to fight, and expected to type. We were a bunch of regular goofballs that shared a common drive to accomplish the mission, and a true love not just for our nation and our occupation, but for each other as well.

## CPT BENJAMIN SMITH

Captain Smith was an infantryman, formally a non-commissioned officer (or NCO) who traded in his stripes for officer bars. He was a ground soldier. He was a real "grunt", one of the rough and tough foot soldiers of the infantry, but he was pretending to be something else. It's easy to tell that he missed his old responsibilities as an infantry platoon leader. He would constantly try to remind whomever would listen that on prior deployments he had served as an infantryman. He got his degree online through Devry University and a few of the other officers in the battalion would tease him about the legitimacy of his education. He was a proud father and a devoted husband. His prized possession was his combat infantry badge earned for exchanging direct fire with the enemy on a previous deployment. He reminded me of an older version of AC Slater from *Saved by the Bell*. This deployment marked his first as an S-1, an office job. He was fair, understanding, happy to teach, and eager to learn.

## SFC THOMAS ANDERSON

Sergeant Anderson was one of the most intimidating men I had ever met. He had eyes that could look right through a man's soul. He wasn't phased by rank. In fact, high-ranking officers feared him. After meeting him at the unit's armory, I knew to keep my distance. His word was the standard in the battalion. If he was on your side, you couldn't be wrong. After a while, his hard exterior broke down, as the understanding developed that his chief motivation was the safety of the troops. He was the best at what he did and he placed the mission first at all times. His dress uniform included awards that had young soldiers in awe. He had done it all. He loved each of us as if we were his own children. I respect him very much. Eventually, when the work was done and the mission complete, he opened up and joked around with us regularly. He was the glue that held our battalion together.

## SSG MATTHEW FASSETTE

Sergeant Fassette got a perfect score on the Army Physical Fitness Test; he was an athlete. He used to be a body builder but slimmed down through increased cardiovascular training. He was dedicated to helping others attain their peak of physical well being through diet and extreme workouts. My favorite thing about him wasn't the fact that he was physically fit, but the method he used to explain concepts. He broke down issues into simple segments so they could be understood with ease. Fassette had deployed once before for service in Kosovo so he was easy to talk to about the complications of deployments and even relationships. He probably wouldn't admit it, but I thought he was a romantic fellow bent on finding love. Though he was single, his two children were the pride of his world.

## SSG MAURICE JASPER

Sergeant Jasper was who every kid wishes his or her dad was—he was just that fun. Jasper was a veteran of Kosovo. Before he joined our section, we were constantly being tasked for various company details in addition to all of our battalion duties. He stood up for us from the start and made our work duties considerably better. He was always cheerful, laughing or joking. His family invited our entire section to join them over the holidays; they were as kind as he was. Yet Sergeant Jasper was extremely opinionated, a feature that drew temporary resentment from soldiers in other sections. He was usually correct though, and if he was wrong he was quick to admit it.

## SSG TONY REITZ

Sergeant Reitz was, like me, a Thiel College alumnus. Reitz technically wasn't a member of our section—he was a one-man section. He served as the chaplain's assistant, making him the personal assistant and bodyguard to Lt. Colonel Etters, a Presbyterian Chaplain. Sergeant Reitz was a people person; everyone liked him. He had three young boys at home and a wife, all of whom he cared about very deeply. Sergeant Reitz was my go-to guy. If I ever needed to complain about something or share the latest gossip, he was there to do it with me.

## SGT JUSTIN ADAMOWICZ

Sergeant Justin Adamowicz was a year older than me and was the easiest to relate to. He was my roommate and best friend in Iraq. He had many hilarious stories to tell and we shared similar tastes in movies. Justin attended Edinboro University but didn't finish, largely because of the military. He was so incredibly intelligent. Before this particular deployment, he had been mobilized and had given support as a member of the National Guard when Hurricane Katrina hit Louisiana. Justin was the least intimidating guy around, a computer geek. He knew his software and multimedia, and was proficient at Excel. I can't help but think how good of a drill sergeant Adamowicz would make. He could be tough but had a gentle demeanor and dedicated himself to the material. Justin remains my dear friend.

## SPC CHARLES PEARSON

Pearson tried the military in his younger days, got out, and came back years later to give it another go. At 41 years of age, he held the rank of specialist. This frustrated him and he felt he deserved more. In the active duty Army it might be strange to have someone that age in that pay grade, but in reserve components that was the norm. The National Guard uses a strict slot-based promotion pyramid in which you can't move up to the next rank until a vacant position exists within your career field. This means that you can get tied up in the same place for a very long time, possibly the duration of your enlistment. (Slots are an invitation for corruption at the battalion level because they promote favoritism over competency. Even if I become an officer, for instance, the potential for advancement is limited compared to active duty.)

Pearson was a good guy. He had two kids, a wife, a MySpace page instead of the popular Facebook, and a Husky dog named Niko. He talked about his dog all the time; he was a true animal lover. Like myself, Pearson spent the deployment learning the 42A (Combat Human Resources) job.

## SPC RICHARD GRIFFITH

Grif was hard for me to understand so he's difficult for me to explain to you. He was a hard worker and had a good heart, but would do anything to impress people in leadership positions and that sometimes presented an issue. If I say I have a Ford, he's got a Mercedes. If you bought a house, he owns a bigger one. When he heard that I went to Thiel, he boasted he earned a doctorate from Westminster College in a year, an impossible feat as Westminster College didn't even offer post-graduate studies at the time. He didn't lie to be malicious; he just wanted desperately to be seen as impressive. At twenty, he was the youngest soldier in our section. He had a young daughter at home and was married to a girl who was raising his daughter along with her own child from a prior relationship. The whole thing reminded me of a bad episode of Jerry Springer. There was a lot of drama with Griff. Despite all of that, I liked him from the start. When he matures though and learns to not always put himself first I think he will be a great soldier. Once I understood why he did things the way he did, I couldn't fault him for it. He had more potential than any soldier in our battalion and we all loved him.

## SPC BRADLEY MCDONALD

Brad was a prior service soldier who came to the Army after a stint as a combat medic with the United States Air Force. He was the first person from the 1-112TH to treat me like a member of the team. He had a wife and kid at home, and came from a musical family himself. His father was a music teacher and he loved to sing, forcing this habit onto Brad. I saw him sing more than I probably cared to. Outside from singing he had a funny way of walking, talking, and throwing a party. It's a difficult thing to "party" in a war zone. Brad would somehow obtain cans of non-alcoholic beer, a stringed instrument, and whatever trash he could find and use it to change what was otherwise a rough looking place into what might roughly translate to a cigar bar night club in a place like war torn Iraq. He was a fun guy. Brad was extremely good at carpentry and woodwork. He took tremendous pride in being a "redneck", a good ol' country boy that knew how to have fun.

## SGT MICHAEL SULLIVAN

Sulli joined us later in the deployment and acted largely as both a unit photographer and mail handler. He was originally from Indiana and had formerly deployed to Iraq. He had been re-called involuntarily to join us on our deployment under a process which has since been discontinued known as "Stop Loss". Sulli was the only liberal in our section and rubbed some people the wrong way occasionally, but I saw him as a true asset; he and I had a great working relationship. I especially appreciated his desire to better himself.

Each of these guys became family to me within a short time. I trusted them all with my life and they trusted me in return. Throughout all of the stress and the tears and the heartache, they were there. When family and home were unreachable, they were there. And, like family, sometimes when you didn't want them, they were there. We were together 24/7. We exercised together, worked together, ate together, and lived together. Not that you could ever sneak off and be by yourself because it wasn't safe to do so (and there was nowhere to go even if you did.) We were in a very dangerous place together during a new and turbulent time. From the very beginning to the very end, no one ever knew or had the foresight to anticipate what would happen next. These men were there every step of the way and I will love them forever.

# EVERY BATTLE
# MATTERS

**M**Y FIRST REAL EXPERIENCE in politics was in the infantry battalion. Over the next few months I would learn the art of debate not in the classroom, but in the barracks. Being true to my history major beginnings, I'm always up to the challenge of defending my beliefs and my scruples. Things aren't always black and white, but sometimes the difference between right and wrong is absolute. So when one of the soldiers in our battalion decided to debate me on historic affairs, I stood up to the challenge. When you are bored, a good debate goes a long way in breaking the boredom. There were many verbal and physical confrontations that would break out, not because we actually cared, but because life was so often mundane and boring.

This soldier insisted that the militia was formed to serve the United States and that singular purpose has been its only aim: to serve a single, centralized federal government. I asked him where the militia was founded. He replied at the Plymouth Bay Colony in 1637, citing a published Army colonel as his source. If the militia was indeed founded to serve a central government, how could it do so at a time when there was no United States at all and national identity was primarily nonexistent? How could an organization be created to serve a country that didn't even exist yet? The colonies were possessions of the British Empire. They were British subjects and willfully submitted to the English Crown. Still, he disagreed and the majority in my unit thought that he made much more sense than I did.

He went on to claim that the United States has been in existence since Pangaea 6,000 years ago and that it's perfectly acceptable for Amish people to wear bright colors, drive convertibles, and listen to iPods (most Pennsylvanians like myself know this to be not the case.) He believed that dinosaurs were not real and that museums perpetuate a great anti-Christian hoax. This guy was a loon to say the least. But the sad fact of the matter is that, in the world we live in, you don't have to be right if you can argue well. I decided to stay clear of him throughout the deployment.

In this unit, many men lied about having gone to college. I suppose they believed it gave them some status or made them feel like they were as good as the officers. I learned how to speak to and influence hard-working people with very real issues in life. Learning to argue about such stupid things on an everyday basis molded me into a leader of influence. I wouldn't again argue with the guy who didn't believe in dinosaurs, but there would be many more arguments with other people. I came to understand that in the infantry you had to either physically fight for what you wanted, or articulate it well enough to convince the commanders that it was essential to doing your job. Put simply, I learned how to barter, and I learned out to bullshit. Both of these skills would serve me well for many years following the deployment.

My job as battalion staff entitled me full access to everyone's files. My secret security and HIPPA clearances both bound me to secrecy but also allowed me insight into my fellow soliders' lives, something the vast majority of the soldiers could not claim. I knew everything about them. I knew where they lived, their education level, how many kids they had, their past criminal indulgences, and even their blood types. Every soldier was a walking novel free for me to read, if only I desired to take the time. I didn't take the time to do so very often.

Many but not most of my compatriots were failures as members of the human race, or at least that's what they would call them on an elite college campus. All my friends were heathens. I loved them anyways. The leadership was no better, however their education and qualifying experiences were always well documented compared to that of the average enlistee.

I was just as educated as most of our officers were with more experience than any of our second lieutenants. I was promised that by that point in my life I'd be an officer myself. Instead, I hadn't even had the chance yet. I found myself now deploying as a sort of honorary grunt—the lowest of the low—and I felt bitter in having to admit that for a long time (in fact, I didn't take pride in it until after the deployment.) And yet here I was, essentially overqualified. I would find the college wrestling team captain within me trying to escape. That Walt was a leader. That Walt saw a direct correlation between hard work and success. That Walt had his issues, but was recognized for his struggles to overcome them. I wanted power and greater responsibility but at every pass I was further reminded that this was not my unit. No promotion slots existed here for me. I was only there because an entire brigade couldn't come close to filling their line-up and I wasn't the only one in this position. Here, I was Junior Varsity. Many other backfills were acting in slots below their rank.

This unit couldn't feel like home. Could anywhere? I was changing. Depression was becoming part of who I was.

What better way to release stress than modern Army combatives, the military's version of mixed martial arts. In a large, saw dust-filled, circular ring we practiced our art form. Just like wrestling with one great exception—the purpose isn't to pin your opponent's shoulders to the mat. Rather, the ultimate goal is to kill your enemy, break your enemy, or hold your enemy off long enough for your back-up to arrive and kill him. Who wins the fight? The man whose battle buddy shows up first with a gun wins the fight.

After learning the Army's level one movements, we wrestled. I was taken back to my college experience doing double legs, cement mixers, and head locks. By the end of the day I was sore, but I was still undefeated after over 100 short combative bouts. Some of the guys there were amazed that a big guy like me could be as agile as I was. I'm not particularly athletic or tough but I've been wrestling long enough for my reactions to be second nature—so I won. Then I won again and again and again. I know my coaches from Thiel would have been impressed, or at least proud. If I bled, I kept fighting. I never quit or gave up my position. I knew without doubt that I had proven myself to many of the infantrymen there. What could they possibly say? I just gave them a free lesson in grappling. I knew that statistically it was a matter of time before I messed up or someone with more skills came along and taught me a lesson but it had not happened yet. I had finally earned the respect of some of the guys and acceptance into the world of the infantry. At the end of the day, I was still stressed out and on edge but I was pleased to have made a positive impression on some of the troops. Maybe I could keep it up. I finally belonged to a group of rejects who were just like me.

Our last days at Camp Shelby were much different than our first in that they were mostly saturated with either training or packing.

The training would have been mostly enjoyable if it weren't for the fact that we had to deal with an active component Army unit who was responsible for rating our battalion on two major training events: detect and defeat IEDs (mounted) and the combat mounted convoy patrol. We rode in Bowheads—Hummer-style vehicles upgraded and modified with scrap iron and plywood to better resemble the M1151 up-armored Humvee.

The IED training served to instill paranoia in soldiers while in transit from one point to another in unfamiliar or hostile terrain. There was no way to win. Even when our dismounted soldiers spotted a training round or IED, the cadre from the First Army demanded we continue, and blew it up anyways. Afterwards we were all heavily criticized by that same cadre for how we attacked each situation. It was lose-lose and largely, for lack of better words, the exercise was bullshit, particularly due to the raters' disrespect towards our chain of command both in formation and during after-action reviews. The hatred towards the First Army grew by leaps and bounds. At one point a grader-sergeant screamed at our company commander, Captain Bill Grosinski, shouting, "You're not listening, sir!" Many of us thought that one of our E-7's would actually have a full-on fistfight with one of the First Army Division cadre if their disrespectful behavior continued.

Despite it all, there were some very good instructors and points made that could save our lives. One captain particularly struck a chord with me when he said during an IED lecture, "There are no more stupid insurgents left because we have already killed the dumb ones. We are dealing with an extremely intelligent and veteran force with an unquestionable ability to adapt and overcome." We all suspected that the captain was correct in his assumptions.

We were soon on coach buses and on the road to Fort Polk, Louisiana for JRTC Phase II, the next part of our Operation Iraqi Freedom mobilization training. Not a soul was sorry to leave Shelby. As the weather grew colder than Pennsylvanians would expect from the southern part of the country, we found ourselves reminded of home. All that seemed to be missing was the snow. And each one of us was looking forward to a Christmas at home with our families and loved ones.

Fort Polk was a large base in area but all in all there wasn't very much on it. Its greatest asset was that it was home to the 4TH Brigade, Tenth Mountain Division, a light infantry brigade long separated from its Tenth Mountain brothers in Fort Drum, New York. We would only be at Fort Polk for a month's time, which wasn't very long at all. Still, the base very obviously wasn't prepared for us all. We spent our first hours on post watching hoards of construction equipment lay gravel and slowly put up the huge white tents that would serve as our temporary billets until better was available. Better would never actually be made available.

The first few nights proved cold as a generator tasked with providing heat failed. It could have been much worse but we still found room to complain. Living in a warehouse tent that was hastily constructed with upwards to two hundred other men was not exactly sanitary or quiet. A visit to the Brigade Command Element living areas nearly broke my heart. Heated trailers, a Post Exchange store on the living zone, laundry trailers, and plenty of showers accented the hierarchy's living quarters. To top it all off, a small group of majors were huddled around a baggage drop-off area finding ample room to complain about their conditions being inadequate. If my rank and status had permitted me I would have sought one of them out and offered an invitation to spend one night with the 1st Battalion 112TH Infantry Regiment in our giant unheated tent. There were only six showers and four sinks for hundreds of men and our Ranger-qualified battalion commander, Lieutenant Colonel Flanegan, who had either too much pride, experience, or both to complain about the cards our little unit had been dealt. I'm sure we had it easy compared to past generations or more elite units—but we weren't either of those things.

In this extremely stressful environment I found that even little things had a profound emotional impact. For example, the death of one of my two pond turtles back home left me at first in a state of denial wondering if perhaps it was just hibernating (it was, after all, wintertime). Eventually the truth took hold. They were my pets. They were living things dependent on my care for survival. Not being there made me wonder what, if any impact, I could have had on the tiny reptile's fate. Why should that bother me so much when I stood poised to take the lives of other human beings, bodies with real souls?

Furthermore, a convoy training lane exercise further disrupted my confidence in my company leadership. Up until minutes before the exercise began, I had no clue as to what vehicle I belonged in. I found out that I was to be the driver of one M1151 up-armored Hummers. This was exciting news. Perhaps it would mean another opportunity to shine for the company leadership. I found out that I was even to have a special guest on board; Captain Fokus, one of the battalion chaplains, was to join us for the ride. What followed embarrassed me and made me wish I was deploying with the Second Brigade instead.

My company reviewed even the simplest of details. It was basic convoy battle drills broken down to their most elementary level. But something quite unexpected happened as our leadership failed us repeatedly. When I, or anyone, tried to speak up or make a suggestion we were ignored. Our voice was not heard. One NCO in particular ruined the atmosphere in our vehicle. He was an Italian man and an E-7 whom had previously been deployed. He'd recently been relieved of duty as platoon sergeant for one of the line companies and now he was my problem. He was terrible and we still had another day to complete on the mounted training lanes. He would scream random words and run off alone into the woods. No one ever corrected him or fixed the problem, even when in a training scenario he led us right into a mock ambush. I heard a 10TH Mountain soldier say, "These Pennsylvania boys are all going to get killed over there." Having bad people in leadership roles was embarrassing. I wanted to operate at a Special Forces Operations level. Instead I felt like we often looked like cub scouts. Everyone was doing their best, and we were learning and getting better every day, but I worried that we might not be prepared fast enough.

The second day went about the same as the first with one major difference: the amount of realism in the scenarios was now remarkable. We convoyed most of the day around the post through various simulated checkpoints and mock Iraqi villages. Only two units were in our JRTC rotation. The first was us—the 56TH Stryker Brigade. The second was the U.S. Navy's SEAL Team Ten. The SEALS were great to work with, consummate professionals. I wish that I could better take the images in my head and commit them to paper for all to read, but still hypnotized by the magic show that was JRTC, I find myself at a complete loss for words about most things. Also, much of what we were doing to train for deployment cannot be fully discussed at this point in time for reasons of security.

I can tell you that there were many actors involved in these drills. After a mock explosion the actors, literally former soldiers, theatre students from local colleges and Middle Eastern refugees were immediately covered in all types of fake blood and gore that would probably make George Romero (of zombie cinema fame) cringe. In many cases there was simply no possible way to win. The exercise ended for me when I was attacked by an actor with a stick-like grenade. Afterwards I was mock-medically evacuated via Stryker and flown away on one of the 1st Cavalry's Blackhawk helicopters. The best part of the exercise was the after-action review (AAR). Our trainers had been videotaping us all day. The NCO that had messed up so terribly for my gun truck was caught on tape again and again screwing up. It was a hilarious cap to the day and an act of karma. I don't want to make myself seem like the perfect soldier; I was far from it. I messed up multiple times and on a daily basis, and I was out of shape compared to many of the soldiers. But I guess that was the point of being there; I was learning how to go to war in the only way the Army knew to teach me.

Though we'd been living in tents without significant heat since we first arrived at Fort Polk, there was much anticipation for the ten-day combat exercises that were about to begin. I began to realize that by staying in positive spirits I could help motivate those around me to rise to any occasion. The more we laughed the more relaxed we were, which meant greater unit cohesion and a much better work environment. I even I bought a lightsaber. That's right—a symbol of the cultural icon that is *Star Wars*. Truth be told I have always been much more of a *Star Trek* fan than a *Star Wars* fan but in the Army the 'Trekkies' are largely outnumbered. We'd been doing a good deal of night ranges and were lacking in entertainment, and since *Star Wars* toys were so inexpensive and readily available I made it a habit to carry the retractable Darth Vader lightsaber and use it to confuse our instructors or the actors playing our opposition. It was most effective as a light wand for traffic and checkpoint operation drills. The toy lightsaber actually does the same job (perhaps better) as the wand included in the standard Escalation of Force kits and at seven dollars it was less than 1/50TH of the price. The prop more than accomplished the desired effects. Most prevalently it got people talking. They all saw in training this chubby young specialist yielding a lightsaber.

I constantly reminded myself that someday, with luck, I would have earned the right to finally call myself an officer even though I had my doubts of the Army's intentions of living up to their initial promises of a commission after all I had been through. Only time would tell. Until then, I carried my *Star Wars* lightsaber until folks in my command advised me that it was not appropriate. I had it for 6 total days, which is 5 days longer than I thought it would take for them to correct me.

# THANKSGIVING

**T**HANKSGIVING SAW US in a new area on the base. The convoy to get there took nearly two hours to complete. We didn't have to move from our other FOB at all. In fact, our brigade was against the decision, but our ranger qualified battalion commander, LTC Flanagan, had plans of his own. The move could have been to impress the visiting adjutant general, but no one really knew. Regardless, we all found ourselves in a new area. This one was void of all cellular reception, which meant that all of the troops, including myself, were hindered from calling our loved ones at home for holiday greetings. The tent was much like the last one but with a major exception— this one had tiny holes scattered around the roof. We all prayed that the rain would hold off for ten more days. Without enough water immediately available to shower or shave, our leadership quickly came to realize that this Thanksgiving adventure was a mistake.

Thanksgiving Day saw a few scattered work details but all in all we didn't do all that much. I think of it now as our first day off since September but I suspected it was a last ditch effort by our command cell to protect themselves from having some private complain to the general of our circumstances. It was a new Army, complaints happened (and apparently were all too common).

The Air Force attachments that would join us for roughly one third of our deployment received all sorts of extra pay incentives for having to deal with all of us. The Air Force folks joined us to support communications and administrative efforts, but in reality we were training them. The people that were attached to us weren't very good at their jobs, but I'm sure that what they learned with and from us would hold tremendous value when they took it back to their home units. When an Air Force Unit is embedded with an Army unit, they regularly receive additional pay and often other benefits as well. They seemed to have it very good. We envied them, and hated them all at once. Apparently their value to the government was far greater than our own, as they had the option of finding more adequate housing and received hardship pay all courtesy of Uncle Sam and the American taxpayer. The airmen decorated themselves well. Each of them wore tabs like those of the Army Ranger saying their specialty and wore airborne wing styled badges just for doing their jobs, or at least that's how an Air Force staff sergeant explained it to me. They even inflated their titles. An Air Force staff sergeant is not of the same pay grade as an Army staff sergeant.

I apologize for complaining but the emotion that goes into mobilization is nearly indescribable and to complain is, at its base, an essential component of human nature. If you have been reading to this point and find yourself saying, "Damn, this is just one long bitch, piss, and moan fest," then you might as well stop reading now because I promise you there will be much more complaining as the story evolves. Think of the complaining more as a critique of my command structure and situational predicaments. I'm not saying that our leadership sucked. I'm also not saying that I could do any better if thrust into their shoes.

Everyone makes mistakes. It should be our priority to learn from both error and success. I am just saying that I should have joined the Air Force!

Use these pages for that purpose—to learn. I don't think the American public really understands that there are all these soldiers in the Army that, like myself, are not designated as combat arms. Sure it's true that every soldier is a rifleman first. If fate were to drive me to it, I would take a human life, though I prayed sincerely that it might spare me such action. I was in an infantry unit but I was not an infantryman. I was a member of the Adjutant General Corps, the oil that keeps the Army's gears running smoothly. Personnel tracking, awards, leaves and passes, pay issues, family issues, and all of the miscellaneous functions that help the ground troops fight the good fight was my problem. It was the essence of my very job. Still, this pre-deployment training served a great purpose. No matter what corps I might be a part of in Iraq, Afghanistan, or any of the other combat zones around the world, I was still an American soldier, and with an American flag on my shoulder I was both a target for the enemy and an ambassador of my country's values. I had no doubts that the enemy would try to kill me as such. There are those in this world whom you have never met and they hate you because you live in America. Every ounce of their being is devoted to the destruction of Western Civilization.

It was a hard truth to face, especially on a holiday dedicated to thankfulness and charity. That being said, back at home Grandma always had a Thanksgiving tradition: amidst trays of turkey and stuffing, cranberries and yams, we would always go around the table each expressing one thing that we were thankful for. This year there wasn't any turkey. There were no smiles, save for some misguided laughs here and there. I thought to myself what I would say if Gram could have asked me what made me thankful this year. I was grateful to be an American soldier, in good health, and with such a strong support system behind me. I'm glad I got my college degree when I did and made the friends that I have. I'm so thankful that I have loved and been loved in return by so many people. I knew that Iraq was waiting and filled with sand and emptiness. I prayed that with time I could maintain a worldview through a child's eyes and that my heart, unlike the desert, could resist filling with heat and dust. Even now, back in the States, I catch myself sometimes looking off into the brush. My thousand-yard stare lasts a little bit longer each time. It wasn't necessarily generated from war, but rather from bullshit. That Thanksgiving, I hoped things would get better, reminding myself that things could always be worse.

Things would get better. They had to. Our actual JRTC evaluation phase lasted a little over a week's time. It began with an array of vehicles: Strykers, Humvees, LMTVs, and Wolfs. There was another move, then another. It became so redundant that in keeping my journal it often felt like I was writing the same events over and over again. Repetition is a wonderful way to train soldiers, but doesn't always make for exciting reading. The trek to our new living quarters took nearly two hours. We arrived to yet another tent. This one had gaping holes in the roof. Regardless of conditions, this training was without a doubt the most involved and realistic that I have had the pleasure of experiencing in my short military career. Real "ghost towns" sprang to life as an array of Arabic-speaking actors moved in. It was an immaculate soap opera laid out before us. Before the evaluation began we got to see the living conditions of Navy Seal Team 10, the other component going through this training. It was easy to see why they were so feared.

Outside of their trailer were stacks of free weights, weight benches, elliptical machines, and stationary bikes. It was like they had a mobile Gold's Gym. It made most of us envious. They knocked out pull-ups like it was nobody's business. We wouldn't admit it openly but it was obvious that these sailors were physically superior to our Rangers. Lieutenant Egan, a Ranger and the platoon leader for our recon platoon, didn't look all that intimidating.

He was a pretty funny guy with more hair on his back than on his head. He declined living in the officer's barracks to live in a tent with his men, an act that did not go unnoticed by his troops. But in doing so, one night in the tent with him led to an interesting reaction from his men. As he removed his shirt, everyone in the tent screamed, "Kill it! Get that thing!" as they saw the hair on his back. I thought there was a snake loose in the tent. It was all pretty hilarious. Lt Egan is one soldier who knew how to get the job done. In this way he was more valuable to our battalion than any SEAL could be.

Another great officer was my own—Lieutenant Benjamin Smith. LT, as I called him, was infantry to the core. You could sometimes tell that his new staff position brought him grief and that he would much rather be out there in the field with his troops. He was a tall soldier with a tan skin tone, claiming Native American heritage. A geek at heart, LT was an avid reader and enjoyed science fiction and horror, especially vampires. He introduced me to the writings of Anne Rice and could sit for hours and tell you all about the habits of the mythical blood suckers. He was so convincing about the doctrine of vampires that sometimes I had to pull myself back to reality and tell myself that they did not actually exist. LT was the public affairs officer for our battalion. This duty required him to babysit the press on training missions.

When my lieutenant, Lt Smith, asked for a volunteer to help him with the press I was quick to raise my hand. Apparently I did an okay job as he later told me that, when his duties required him to leave the wire in Iraq, he would take me with him if that were my wish. I assured him that it would be my honor to do so.

More and more of Iraq was being handed over to native Iraqi forces every day. It was expected that we would leave Al Taji midway through our deployment to take up residence in a makeshift base. It was also whispered that Iraqi operations might be reclassified as a United Nations peacekeeping mission sometime while we were there.

Our battalion had grown much closer in the last few months. With Christmas rapidly approaching, spirits began to rise. We traded out our civilian caterers for Army cooks. We probably had the best field feeder team in the entire brigade. The improvement in chow happened almost overnight. I believe it was Napoleon who first said, "An Army marches on its stomach". If this is true, and I believe it is, then we should have crushed through Bagdad with all the power of an over-sized steamroller. The food was good, to say the least.

After JRTC had officially ended, the process of packing and loading for our next destination began. Over the months I had learned how to get very good at packing a lot of items into a small space.

A recurring trend became more apparent, one that made me irate. Our company began to shit all over us, the S-1 section. The First Sergeant was always quick to choose members of the S-1 shop (my section) for various details and undesirable missions. It was obvious that he disliked us from the beginning. I'm not exactly sure why this was so but I strongly expect that it is because we could not identify as combat arms. The First Sergeant, Top as we called him, was a great guy, but we were staff pukes to him. We were an oddity in a primarily infantry company. The company looked at us and said, "Those guys aren't pulling their weight". And so we were always picked first for the worst details. I cleaned weapons systems that the company wouldn't let me operate. I cleaned shower trailers and did KP duty all while lower ranking soldiers slumbered in their bunks. I was grateful that peeling potatoes was no longer done in the Army. Nobody was standing up for us. There was a good reason we weren't always visible to the HHC Company; we were, quite literally, off doing other things.

As a battalion element we were responsible for four companies in total. We belonged to one of those companies only because we had to belong to someone. It's just the way things were. This meant that when Christmas leave was near, everyone became my problem. We had to track and log the leave for every individual member of each separate company, put every soldier in those perspective companies in for any awards that they were due, pick up and deliver mail, make additional I.D. tags for soldiers with less than four sets...long story short, it was one of our busiest times. Yet no one recognized us at all. No medals or awards for us, the non-infantry, not even a silent applaud or pat on the back for doing the most important job in the modern military—taking care of soldiers. An unhappy soldier is a less effective soldier. Eventually a new First Sergeant, Larry Deal, helped to ease some of the tensions. I never knew what came of the old Pathfinder First Sergeant.

I almost laughed when I saw a recommendation for an Army achievement medal pass by my desk for one company's "unit administration NCOs". The sergeant nominated was a good guy and an infantryman, a former member of the elite 75TH Ranger Regiment. What got me was that the given reasons for him getting the award weren't things that he did, they were things that my section did but would never be recognized for. I couldn't believe it.

I would never receive an Army achievement medal, one of the military's most basic awards. Like I said, the NCO up for award was a great soldier and a stand-up guy. He was also essential to the unit. But there were failings in that company. We were not adequately informed of changes to his company's numbers before our daily strength reports and most of the time it was us who told them who was on leave and why. I hoped that our leadership might take notice of what my section was doing.

Everyone had the opportunity to go to the Post Exchange (PX) for haircuts and personal hygiene items except for us until one sunny morning. Even then, we had to gear up, putting on our Kevlar helmets and use a tactical armored vehicle for transport because an NCO in another section somehow believed that his guys deserved to use the battalion van more than us, though it had been our responsibility to track vans throughout the entire mobilization. The S-1 section was responsible for the vans. We signed for them. We had to know where they were, but we could never actually use them for our own missions. It was extremely frustrating.

We couldn't get haircuts or soap bars but later that day the van magically appeared with a Sam's Club load of soda and candy to be sold for a marginal profit. That's way more important than me having toothpaste, isn't it? The small town politics like those of my little hometown of Aspinwall existed even here, in a place so many miles away from home and with so many different kinds of people. Yet rewarding the undeserving was, as much as I hated it, an integral part of my job.

It's funny that people can make such a huge deal out of what medals a senator threw away in Vietnam, or why a Japanese-American from World War II didn't get his due awards. It's just a piece of metal. I didn't always think that way. Once upon a time, winning a wrestling match for a bronze medal meant everything to me. Even silver or bronze meant I had excelled where others had tried and failed. I love getting recognized to this day but I have to admit that I haven't been recognized like I would have liked since college. I've found that the absence of glory has a profound effect on how I carry myself. I don't act like a champion because that's not typically how I feel most of the time. Again, things weren't always that way. I feel like the old man telling his grandkids about walking in the snow, without shoes, uphill both ways to school every day when I talk about my recent past.

I am from that trophy generation. The Army taught me that I wasn't special or exceptional. It is a good lesson, but I still contend that it is incorrect—I am very special. I will change this world.

I was a warrior until I joined the Army. The wrestler in me struggles to keep my back from being pinned to the floor but it's hard. I noticed my body getting older a little more each day. Without being able to work out every day I felt like I was terribly fat, even though I had no clue what I actually weighed in those days. There were no scales around. It wasn't a healthy way to live and I knew I was going to have to find a way to fix it or the next great ordeal would probably drive me to insanity. I was caught somewhere between heaven and hell and I often found myself conflicted, praying for love and yearning for war.

# THE WAR WITHIN

**T**HINGS WERE GETTING WORSE by the day in Afghanistan and the rest of the world wasn't faring much better. The Russian fleets were sailing the seven seas again and looking for trouble in Latin America, as countries like Venezuela contracted to purchase arms. It looked as though the Cold War ways might come back as an obvious cycle of Westernized warfare continued. Tensions in other Middle Eastern countries like Egypt and Libya, ensured that our military would have a very busy future, perhaps needlessly so. I didn't understand how life at home could go on when the world was on fire. I felt very much alone, and sometimes saw being alone as preferable as the Army had succeeded in convincing me that evil existed. It was real.

And yet in all of this, my friend Kayla was going to get married. Kayla was a girl that I went to college with and we remained good friends. She was an extremely talented student, much more so than myself. We had our fair share of ups and downs, though the ups definitely outweighed the downs. One night in college when alcohol, peer pressure, and boredom came together, I said some things to her that I probably never should have. The result was half a year of her not speaking to me. She felt that I was the worst person in the world for what I said. Yet the next year she did something really amazing that completely shocked me—she completely forgave me. This act speaks volumes about the type of person she is and the type of person I hoped I could be. Perhaps it was the ease of summer, or maybe she even suspected that deep down I was really sorry. Whatever the reason, she forgave me. I really cared about her. I guess I was partially lamenting not having a relationship of my own, or perhaps just regretting some of the things I'd done in the past. I was growing up. Her and I weren't ever in a relationship, but I thought I'd come close a couple times. I had some weird feelings about missing out.

Slowly but surely our friendship healed. We went back to being friends and were stronger than ever. When she started dating a sailor in the Navy I had to rib her a bit. Once upon a time, I felt I belonged in the Navy, but now I was a soldier, a warrior, and a member of the Army. Kayla's beau was stationed in Hawaii and I quickly saw that he was a nice guy. Despite the distance between them, they seemed to overcome and prevail. For Christmas one year, he gave her an engagement ring. I was happy for her but suddenly started feeling more and more alone. It seemed as if all of my friends, male and female, from both high school as well as college, were getting hitched.

The thought of marriage and "settling down" seemed comfortable to me but also somehow puzzling. A long-term, serious relationship seemed to be, in reality, more difficult than the alternative. I was starting to look at Army life as resisting the natural order of things. In an infantry unit without females, the aim shifts from being happy to just surviving. I have a million Kayla stories—missed opportunities because I didn't step up to the plate—from Army Anna, who couldn't date seriously until she finished a medical degree (at least eight years away at her rate), to Wrestling Amber, who never quite had the right opinion or the true story. From Backstreet Brynnly who grew up with me (and I imagine would be the "coolest" girl a guy could have), to Slutty Shana (obvious one), love never seemed to go right for me. I was having deep thoughts about my love life, perhaps because there were no women in my infantry unit I was just missing a female presence in my life. I'm sure that a big part of that is me, my personality, and how and where I grew up. I'm not a player at all. Rather I'm a thinker and in some part a hopeless romantic. It's not at all uncommon for me to slip off into a daydream and wonder what things could be like for me if I would have done things just a little bit differently. The whole world would have been different. Then again, it was a girl cheating on me that was my greatest motivation for losing weight and overcoming an eating disorder and it is that weight loss that paved the way for me to become a military man. There were reminders, often from unlikely places, that I was loved. For example, a high school student from New Jersey named Alannah wrote me letters every week and mailed me sour patch kids on a regular basis, essentially sponsoring me. There were many people like Alannah, who were at the time strangers, which showed me extreme kindness and support for what I was doing, despite not really knowing me.

Now I can honestly say that I've done just about everything that my society views as the essence of being a man. I've been a successful collegiate wrestler, a veteran firefighter, and now a soldier. What could I possibly do next? All I could think of after Iraq would be the obvious: a steady career, a home, and most important of all, a family.

Being a father would mean a chance to do better than my own father did. An opportunity to take a young life and mold it to greatness would be incredible. I knew that I was nowhere near ready for so big a step in my life. Some argue that the fear of doing poorly would make me a good parent. I just didn't know and, being single, it was too much for my brain to think about at the time. I practiced being a dad in my own way—by taking care of my soldiers. It wasn't always the simplest task but it was mine as a human resource specialist and as a human being. These guys were my responsibility.

In some ways I was glad I wasn't married. There was a myth within our unit that all Army women were basically whores. Of course this is not true. There are some very nice women serving in the U.S. military. However, it is easy to see how the perception developed and personally I'm not sure I'd be quick to date a girl that has seen a combat zone. I wouldn't want to compete with the attention they received in the military (this is an insecurity of mine, and not a reflection on them). So many girls from the support battalions put out that they earned themselves a good reputation. Guys would actually know what female soldiers to go to, by name, for "service". Fortunately for the girls, the brigade distanced the testosterone-driven infantry units like ours from theirs. The unit withheld so many privileges from us that when we finally got to have some, it really did feel a bit like Christmas. It's just as simple to forget how to deal with the opposite sex. I don't mean to minimize the female contribution to the war effort. Many women are heroes, but I served during a time when the role of the female soldier to the organization was still being figured out by the organization at large and many of the leadership was sexist.

In my own pursuit of a relationship however, I felt lost. Once upon a time I was a remarkable Casanova. I always thought it was funny that my friend Joey would always try to pick up women online. At websites like Facebook, Myspace and HotOrNot.com, all the cards were laid out on the table for him to see. He selected females on strict criteria from looks to general interest. I always looked at this hobby of his as if he were a loon. "That's crazy," I would tell him. "Why don't you just go out to a church, bar or a club?"

I always thought it was sad but now I understand better where Joey was coming from. He was just lonely. And in a world where relationships are so seemingly competitive, you had to have something special to offer that would distinguish you from the rest of the crowd. Take that same stance and apply it to the U.S. military (not even just the all-male combat arms groups). The statistics tighten down even more. There are even fewer available women than there are in the Pittsburgh scene. With Christmas leave only a week away I did what Joey did and got online, only to get offline about 45 seconds later. It was stupid and to me it wasn't at all worth the loss of dignity. I thought I'd just try it my way when I got back to Pittsburgh. Maybe I was just meant to be alone? The thoughts flooded my mind. I've always been a thinker. My mind is a super-collider of insanity. I think that I was focusing on relationships, or anything, to distract myself from what was coming. Iraq was coming. A war was in my future.

The soldiers said that Iraq was getting worse, but the media pushed the narrative that Iraq looked to be getting safer. An Internet news site had a humorous story. It seemed that our Commander-in-chief, President George W. Bush, thought the time was right for a diplomatic visit to the now nation of Iraq. While sitting down with local leaders, a projectile was launched from across the room. It wasn't a bullet or a mortar—it was a shoe. A disgruntled Iraqi man was apparently so angered by the President's visit that he removed his shoes and tossed them at the President's head. If the President wouldn't have flinched and moved to evade it, he would have been bruised. Even without being struck, the act bruised his dignity, I am sure. This also showed that the world was growing much less fearful of the U.S.

Regardless of how people feel personally or politically, disrespecting our Commander-in-chief is disrespecting us, our presence, and our compassion towards the Iraqi people. I felt that this act should not have been tolerated and that those involved should have been dealt with by the harshest means possible.

The Middle East was obviously unhappy with the forced peace brought on by our presence. According to the soldiers that had been there, Iraq was not settling down like the media tried to make it look. Things were actually getting worse.

A brief article in the *Army Times* cited an intimidating phenomena occurring in the Mosul region of Northern Iraq. Apparently, people wearing Iraq Army (IA) uniforms had been attacking American military personnel. The article didn't mention whether those involved were or were not actual IA soldiers. What it did say is that this tactic had had some success, killing several Americans and wounding others in the few instances in which it had been attempted. I was sure this would incite mass fear and paranoia at Taji if it were ever to occur. Camp Taji was already staffed over fifty percent by the IA. Half of the base was theirs. In my eyes this meant that there would be no shortage of military surplus available to the enemy, whomever it might have been. The threats that my unit would face were evolving. The enemy was trying new things. On a lighter side, half of everything I heard that pertained to my status in the military was secondhand information circulated primarily through gossip. This meant that most of the time you heard about a formation or detail from your peers rather than from your chain of command. This led to a whole lot of misinformation and rumors. Some of it surprised and gripped me when it ended up being true. The latest holiday rumor was that we'd all be under the 82nd Airborne Division in Iraq rather than the 1st Cavalry Division. From what I gathered this would be most certainly be a positive change. Who knew if it was true?

# INDIANTOWN GAP

**A** WEEK LATER I WAS done with the South—no more Camp Shelby or Fort Polk. I had passed training and was rubber-stamped for overseas service. I now found myself in the mighty Union and, just like the Pennsylvanian soldiers of 1862 who endured below that great battle line now called the Mason Dixon, I was glad to be back in the hands of the North. My battalion flew into McGuire Air Force base in New Jersey on a civilian Boeing 747.

The airmen there were pretty funny. You could tell that the thrown-together force took their jobs just seriously enough to try to impress whichever military group would step off the plane. With their newly issued Tiger-stripe ABU uniforms they were an easy target for jokes but they were largely spared because so many of our guys were extremely tired. We were beat down from the months of poor leadership decisions, learning, and growing pains. Like zombies we marched towards Christmas in a haze. My main hope was that we learned something from most of our many deficiencies.

One thing I do know is that I loved Fort Dix. Fort Dix was an Army base in New Jersey, in the north. This was one of the posts that we would stop at prior to Christmas leave. This is surprising because everyone had said how terrible it was going to be. To me however, the facts outweighed the rumors. We had hard barracks (brick buildings) instead of tents that were similar to what I had lived in at Advanced Individual Training (AIT), just one-year prior at Fort Jackson, South Carolina. To think we had complained at AIT about things like mold and chipping paint—we must not have known how good we had it. We had hard walls again! No tents! And we got three hot meals a day in a stellar cafeteria (DEFAC). No more pre-packaged Meals Ready to Eat (MREs) meant no more stomach issues for many of the soldiers. We also had running water instead of portable shower trailers and toilets instead of Porta-johns. It's insane how much pleasure one can take in knowing that when he uses the latrine today the shit from yesterday won't still be there. God bless indoor plumbing and thank you Fort Dix!

We were finally being treated more like active duty Army Soldiers should be. We were living in the garrison, saluting when the colors (flag) were raised and lowered, and wearing our uniforms with pride, looking more the part than the other branches that were there. There are so many day-to-day conveniences that Americans take for granted. Yet getting some of them back felt like freedom. (Insert William Wallace Braveheart scream here.) I knew it wasn't true liberty but for the time it was certainly close enough.

With a move from Fort Dix to Fort Indiantown Gap just a few days away we braced for what was to come there. The move was sudden, and certainly not routine for the military, but our command wanted us to be at a base that made it easy for most of us to get home inexpensively, and many of us hailed from Pennsylvania where Fort Indiantown Gap was located. I had originally considered a trip to Fort Bragg, North Carolina to present a now former-girlfriend with a promise ring. It wasn't meant to be. I had been a negative influence on her life and she was a negative influence on mine. I had learned that my mom had another tumor—so I had a very good reason to go home. I wanted to be with my mother.

I didn't have a normal support system in place to deal with this news. In a time and place where communication with the outside world was increasingly difficult, I found myself wishing I had my ex-girlfriend back. But the hard truth of the matter was that, like so many before her, she had abandoned me. I often wonder of ex-girlfriends if they talk about me like I'm a good guy or a psychopath. I've been a little bit of each at times, I think.

I suppose that in hindsight it was a blessing in disguise. Iraq was right around the corner and I found myself alone, my tear ducts drier than the deserts I would soon occupy. Unable to cry amongst my peers, I retreated to my bunk and tried to sleep. My mom, the woman who gave me life, was dying. I tossed and I turned as I thought of the future.

The girl I had broken up with from North Carolina was a pretty girl with a nice smile; her voice kept me calm, but she was a soldier. I knew from the start that she wouldn't last. We met on the trails of Fort Jackson, South Carolina. At first, she was mean to me. Later, jealousy from other soldiers like Bianca of my own division, and Natasha of the Nebraska National Guard set some wheels in motion.

One night while off post we found ourselves in the same room. I was checking my email on my buddy Joseph's computer when she wandered over. "Do you care if I check mine?" she asked. I looked at her intensely and agreed, getting up to relinquish my chair. She grabbed me by the arm and told me I didn't have to get up. She then sat on my lap and started typing, explaining to me her life, showing me pictures of her home and friends, opening up to me completely. The room was filled with other people drinking, laughing, singing and partying. All of those people disappeared. It was only her and I. I had on what we called in Fort Sill our "artillery goggles"—everyone was looking good. With enough time, even the lunch ladies looked good.

The next day she wanted nothing to do with me. I asked her out multiple times. Her answer was always the same: "What's the point Rosado?" I couldn't believe that she could be right. I've always been stubborn. So I pushed for a relationship when I should have yielded to reality. We had ended up together for a while despite her initial response. I suppose I never learned how to pick and choose my battles, and often get emotionally entangled in situations where the best reaction would have been to simply walk away. We kept up a long distance relationship for an entire year, seeing each other more than most couples that live together. It was all going well until I got my Iraq orders and started to mobilize. I began the journey that I am chronicling here and we grew further and further apart. Worst of all, I feel like I pushed her away like I've pushed away everyone that has really cared about me throughout my life. When I was tired, I slept instead of calling her. When she needed me, I wasn't there for her. On the eve of holiday exodus she told me it was over. She'd had enough. I agreed. What we had was not worth fighting for.

Before I had even left for war a part of me was sad. Most people know the feeling that accompanies a breakup. I knew that I had felt it before; I would feel it again. Still there's no way to soften the blow or numb the sting. I didn't know how to cope so I started watching a TV show called *The Office*.

I breezed through the first three seasons in a matter of weeks. I loved the show but it was difficult for me to laugh. Still, every now and then the colorful cast of comedians could get a smile out of me. That second without pain eased my tension. Michael, Dwight, Pam, and Jim, the characters in the show, became my temporary release from the Army. I watched whenever I could. I'd love to thank those actors for giving me some joy in such a dark and emotional time.

Staff Sergeant Jasper lived in Hershey, Pennsylvania (home of the milk chocolate candy bar) and I think he could see that morale was really lacking in our section around this time. His wife, children, and family lived near the fort there, so one night, while his wife's family was hosting a party, he grabbed me and five other soldiers from my section and we crashed it. It was the best food I'd had in three months. They treated us like family. There were children everywhere and each one of them was more than excited to have Army Soldiers at their party. They even gave us all gift bags and made sure that we knew that they were grateful to us for what we were doing. We were equally grateful for the kindness that we were shown.

The atmosphere was crazy; everyone was playing the video game *Guitar Hero*, wrestling, and relaxing. Everything was like it was supposed to be. I realized then that Jasper had built his own family from scratch and had become an integral part of each of their lives. It touched me deeply and once more I allowed myself to dream. I think aging was getting to me. I was starting to wane at only twenty-five years of age. By the end of the night I knew that my plans would not change. I would still go to school and learn more about being a "real" grown up each day, but, somewhere in my heart I wished that I could be a father and an uncle with a huge family where I would be idolized and loved until my dying day. I didn't come from a traditional family, so the idea of it was beautiful to me. With the war inching closer, it dawned on me that I might never get to realize this dream of being accepted. I had done a lot for my age and in some ways the knowledge that I had amassed made my eyes burn and my head sting. Being intelligent and knowing how to think can feel like a terrible curse. Like all dreams, the time comes to wake up sooner than you might want.

It was nearly Christmas and I was one of only a few soldiers left at Fort Indiantown Gap. As a backfill, I was pretty much alone. The soldiers of the company were transported back to their home armory in

Erie on a large bus. I was left to fend for myself. I had rented a car with Brian Dorben and Nick Lehota, two other soldiers from Pittsburgh. We couldn't go to our armory like the organic guys. We were backfills. We had to wait. In declaring an attempt to make us equal to their "good old' boys" the command element of my battalion had separated us all once again. We were the last to go home and it was our responsibility, not the Army's, to get there. Home would be a welcome sight. I tried to think of Jesus—the real reason for Christmas. Would this Iraqi crusade have happened without Jesus?

When I got home I immediately saw that Aspinwall was the same as it had been when I left—a small town that fought with all its nerve to resist change. The fire department didn't seem to be on my side anymore. The fire department had offended me by bagging my gear and giving away my stall. When a fellow firefighter, Mike Sweeney, went to Iraq as a private contractor making near six figures a year, the outcry of support was tremendous; his gear remained in the same place for his year away as if enshrined. I had flashlights and equipment as well as an expensive pair of Warrington Pro leather boots that I had purchased with my own money that were stripped and stolen during my months away. I was an armed soldier making only around $30,000 per year. The offense would impact my level of participation in later years.

The volunteer fire department was an already struggling organization. People weren't showing up for fire calls and they were having major fundraising issues. Like everywhere else, there were people whose goal was self-preservation rather than the good of the community, but there were also a few great people. It would not have been hard to fix the fire department. Running more domestic calls and lowering the call volume would give people a reason to serve. Greater rewards for service would affect morale. Little things that could make all the difference would never get the chance because of a few people that would rather decorate themselves than save a town. They actually gave a huge departmental honor to a kid that could very possibly be considered mentally slow, and who had never stepped foot into a fire because all of the officers saw him as a liability, but lacked the balls to tell him that.

What really got to me was that money, which was so hard to earn through an exhausting fundraising process, was so frivolously spent without consideration. No one wanted to hear anything that might spark change and so the few that really cared were ignored. The fire department was an exact miniature embodiment of the disappointing bureaucracy that was plaguing the federal government.

Obviously, committing these thoughts to paper will not earn me any applause. At best they might earn me some unwanted gossip. In Aspinwall, gossip translates to success. But honesty is what this book is all about. The simple fact of the matter is that, at that point, I didn't care who I pissed off. I found out that the old saying was one-hundred percent true: "It's far better to be pissed off than to be pissed on." My old support system wasn't good enough anymore. I had grown past it. The breakdown of my support system, however, led me to be depressed. This was a condition that was reflected for me in weight gain.

I gained a lot of weight since going to active duty and my depression, as well as my overall experiences so to date, gave me a clear weight-loss goal for the deployment. I wanted to weigh less than 200 pounds and pass the Army Physical Fitness Test. The stress didn't do much for my confidence. I was excited to meet with my friends from school but embarrassed to because of how I looked and how I felt. I was very sad most of the time and it is safe to say that I was looking forward to getting back to the infantry battalion where, even though I wasn't always warm or dry or happy, I did at least have some sense of purpose. My family was broken. My mom was sick. My friends were nowhere to be seen, and my community was pre-occupied.

On the home front, time was rapidly playing catch up. My mother, who was deaf, had cancer again. My uncle who had cerebral palsy had gained weight and now required a breathing machine and a constant flow of oxygen to live any sort of life. My grandma was getting older. She was the one I depended the most on. My brother was struggling to grow up as much as I secretly was, struggling just to make it. My father had long since abandoned me and his side of the family had been absent from the very beginning. With no woman in my life, the position of girlfriend remained vacant and I accepted that I deserved no better. I began to fear the future. It was an unhealthy way to be. I felt like those in my town had forgotten me. The firemen seemed to want nothing to do with me. The only ones who cared enough from my past to visit or call were Marc, Lee, Jared, Jimmy, Joe, and Bryan— true friends. I worried about what would happen in my own family more than I worried about the things happening in my own life.

I had gained back so much of the weight I had struggled so hard to lose and, worst of all, I was undeniably unhappy and depressed. My family did love me and I loved them but there was always that fear inside me. I wasn't a child anymore but I was so far away from achieving adulthood. The inner conflict is difficult to commit to paper. I was disgusted at the monster that stared back at me when I looked into the mirror every day. His baby blue eyes pushed through a face that didn't belong. Short hair nearly matched the stubble on its face. There was anger, but only so much as to cover up the underlying pain. It was fatter than the average soldier but it had a stare that showed all it had endured. I couldn't believe that it was me. I prayed that I could control it. I knew I could not.

Gambling was now legal in our state. I more than partook though I couldn't bring myself to drink again, not even a drop. I had lost my taste for alcohol somehow. I partook in other vices, though. Over Christmas I would often go outside to run. I missed the physical punishment of college wrestling. I felt fat and I tried to punish myself for letting everything I had worked for go in a few months. It was all for not. Nothing I did seemed to matter. I sat in a puddle of my own sweat. I was fat and alone but for immediate family on Christmas. Of course, I wasn't truly alone at all. I was just too narrow-minded and selfish to comprehend that people were supporting me. I spent a lot of quality time with my grandmother; she was always there for me. I can't think of a single exception to this from Cub Scouts to college graduation. She was, is, always has been, and probably always will be my best friend.

A lot of people and personalities seem to flow in and out of my life. It's funny how things turn out. People who you think will be by your side forever disappear. Even the bond of blood can disperse. I've had cousins who were friends and mentors tell me they hated me only to ask to use my truck, or even in a rare case ask me to donate body parts for an operation. The "family thing" to do would be to oblige, but the sensible thing to do is to refuse. I don't require much to be someone's friend. Even honesty can be bent and I tend to remain loyal. Borrowing a line from the film *Striking Distance*, "Loyalty above all else except honor." I wondered how much honor there could be in the mission I was soon to execute.

When you are young you never really comprehend how quickly things will change, or even that they will at all. You look at the elderly as you look at foreigners, like they're some different species that you will never become. At some point in your life you look back and know that the best times are over and that things will never be the same. It's like an early mid-life crisis that people and kids in their twenties tend to have. It probably has something to do with being out on your own, college behind you.

Becoming a working man, forming relationships, and going to war was what was expected of me. But going away to battle changes how people look at you. Everyone tells you to come home alive; usually they're in tears when they do this. People who you never thought held you in any kind of esteem all of a sudden want to shake your hand. The handshake is always soft. It's never firm like that expected of a businessman. Instead they shake with you as if they are shaking hands with death, as if you are some fragile object that will shatter at the slightest roughness. People say thank you but I wonder if they know just what they are thanking us for. Most people don't know what it's like to sleep outside in the cold rain, or low crawl through mud and sand. Most people have not dug their own latrines, fired bullets on their brother man, or left everything and everyone they love behind to defend them and preserve the values of our country. There is so much more to it. It makes you miss the love, warmth, and comfort of being a child. Will that kind of comfort ever come again?

Christmas break was over. It was time to work. I found relief on the road back to post with Lehota and Dorben. I was with my own kind again. I was with people as messed up as I was, soldiers with heavy hearts. As bad as things got and as disappointed as I sometimes found myself feeling, I knew in my bones that I would feel at home with other grunts like me. I suspect if I ever do become an officer, part of me will always be a regular Army grunt at heart. We were all sad and we were all definitely going through issues. It was easy to see that my problems weren't the worst in my company. There were guys whose wives were cheating on them, guys with sons and daughters getting arrested. There were guys whose families were dying in droves and guys with bankruptcy and foreclosure slips. Back on post we were all green. All of us were the same. It was obvious that it wouldn't take long for our volcanic mix to erupt in anger and confusion but for the moment we were all cool characters. Let's let the volcano erupt on the enemy overseas.

# THE FINAL COUNTDOWN

**A** FEW MORE DAYS in Pennsylvania were required mainly as a formality. We ran various ranges, shot all types of weapons, and as S-1 it was our job to complete the long process of signing everyone back in from holiday leave. The new Stryker barracks at Fort Indiantown Gap which we perceived initially to be a blessing, revealed themselves as a curse. The cleaning standards for these barracks were unattainable and unreasonable. Our Division Command wanted to hold us back until the job was done to their standard. The bus company threatened that unless we moved to Fort Dix at the previously scheduled time they might not be capable of transporting us. Our command sergeant major made the decision that we would move on to Dix. Charlie Company was left behind to finish cleaning. The soldiers of Charlie were sucked in to doing the meaningless task of cleaning an already immaculate barracks area. It sucked for them but I was too relieved to be moving on to care. It could have just as easily been my company and I had done enough cleaning over the past months.

In New Jersey we were once again treated to all the luxuries of a former Army basic training site and an active major Air Force base, including a huge Post Exchange (PX) and a bowling alley. Unfortunately my section was tasked out to our brigade element for the duration of our stay. Brigade had failed to accurately complete their task of accounting for soldiers and their medical and admin files, and neglected to verify our proposed flight manifest rosters. They called in the battalions to pick up their slack. Our company-level leadership never seemed to acknowledge all of the extra work that we had to do. I got issued new IOTV body armor, packed my three allotted duffle bags, loaded the bags onto a large truck, boarded a bus, and I was on my way.

When I arrived at McGuire Air Force Base to await an overseas flight, the atmosphere got better. Gail Kasper, former Miss Continental America, was there to send us off. She was a bit older, beautiful to be sure, but what I appreciated most about her was her dedication to all of us. A USO representative assured me that Miss Kasper wasn't paid to be there but that she never missed an outgoing flight of troops. She posed for pictures, signed autographed posters, and boosted all of our morale not because she had to, but because she wanted to. One of the guys whispered to me, "I'd marry that girl". I looked back at him laughingly and said, "Who wouldn't? She's Miss USA for Christ's sake!"

It was easy to see that none of the three general officers or sergeants major that were running the show around our send off had a combat patch on their shoulder. In a year we would have something that they probably never would. We left the reception area and walked outside onto a concrete tarmac. As we stepped onto the huge DC-10 aircraft we started to realize that this was to be our last stroll on American soil for some time. Liftoff marked the end of the mobilization chapter. We were now all officially deployed soldiers with NATO orders in hand.

# DEPLOYED

**T**HE PLANE WAS CRAMMED and heavy. We filed in from rear to front, filling every seat. The lower levels of the aircraft were hunkered down with the bags, additional weaponry, and equipment that we would come to use. Crammed as it was, we all tried to relax. Many slept to pass the time. Three movies were shown: *Iron Man, Indiana Jones and the Crystal Skull*, and *Be Kind Rewind*. Most of us had seen all of the movies already, despite how new they were. Video piracy had become the quid pro quo. Every other soldier had an external hard drive that stored up to hundreds of compressed and bootlegged videos.

The plane smelled of old socks but the attendants did their best to keep us happy by providing us with sodas, meals, and hot towels on request. It took a long while to get up to cruising elevation. The flight remained unchanged pretty much for the whole ride. We put down in Germany, my first time in Europe. When my feet hit the ground I felt a certain pride in where I was. I had made it to the home of some of my ancestors, which I had traced to around the year 1560 in what is today Germany. It's a shame that all I would get to see of the country would be a warehouse next to a terminal.

The warehouse was something in itself, though. The vendors were German and mostly women. I sipped a Coca-Cola but was disappointed at the different formula used by Germany's Coke factory. I stared at rows of German chocolates and clothing. There were t-shirts commemorating the Berlin Wall, and music that was quasi-techno flowed through the air. The big-ticket item was absinthe—a notorious green alcoholic beverage that was illegal in the States at the time. We had all heard stories about the drink's potency. I wanted to buy a bottle but it was forbidden under our orders. Still, I hoped that we would have a chance to stop there on the way home from Iraq. Maybe then I could sneak a bottle in my carry-on.

The Germans had no remorse about taking our money as if we were regular tourists. We were only in the country for a few hours when word came that our plane was refueled, clean, and ready to move out. A group from the 10TH Mountain Division joined us en route to Afghanistan. To me, they offered a glimpse of my future. It was no secret that tomorrow's battles would be waged in mountainous Afghanistan. If I could survive Iraq, Afghanistan was where I would likely go next.

I had a poor concept of time, but after what felt like another several hours on the airplane, I saw a sea of lights shining below. It looked much bigger than Pittsburgh did, even from the air. It was Kuwait City.

Twenty minutes later I was on Kuwaiti soil. It was a cool night and we were quickly loaded again onto large coach buses with blacked out windows. It was a two and a half hour tactical movement via the buses to Camp Buehring. We were armed as a precaution but the official stance was that we were guests in an allied sovereign nation. Kuwait had some of the nicest, most up to date roads and vehicles that I had ever seen. Oil money had been put to use there.

Yet Kuwait was a designated combat zone. There were radical groups attacking convoys with IEDs and small arms fire, but the government did its best to suppress the hostilities. They did so with great effectiveness due of their association (largely business-wise) with the Western world.

Our base in Kuwait was in the middle of a vast desert. There was sand as far as the eye could see in every direction you looked. Strykers were arriving daily. We were joined on the base by the Marines and elements of the mighty British Army. The Englishmen were colorful and funny but they also showed extreme dedication to the war effort. Each morning our revelry bugle call played loudly over giant loud speakers. It was followed in turn by what I thought was their version. The American call was loud and boisterous to wake up soldiers. You could almost visualize Custer charging a group of Plains Indians across an open field on horseback. The British call was much more classical and quite epic, so much that the Americans looked forward to hearing it instead of their own. Men would cheer, "Let's here the Brits call". The English song ended up being the theme from the movie *Patton*, as the Third Army was commanding the post in Kuwait—we were all mistaken. The song wasn't British at all.

I had to attend a class on force recognition taught by an English sergeant. At first he was difficult to fully understand, but he concluded his lecture with an easily comprehensible, "Good luck in Iraq. We'll see you all next year in Afghanistan". There was no mistaking what he said, but we couldn't help but wonder, would we?

The political landscape had changed almost overnight. Iraq was holding elections free of American intervention. It seemed certain that particular militant leaders would seek power through this method. President Bush had promised withdrawal from Iraqi cities by 2011 but Iraq had made it clear that they hoped the day would come sooner. It was doubtful to us that a status of forces agreement with Iraq outlining the future of U.S. involvement in the country would be reached. In some countries, dictatorships work better.

A new face entered the mix as Barack Hussein Obama was inaugurated as the President of the United States. His campaign against John McCain was entertaining to be sure. It was a circus of a campaign covering up real issues. It disgusted me from every angle. I'm a Republican and I couldn't understand why my party wouldn't stand up for what was real. Barack didn't do any better. No one seemed to know who he was. He was a man without a real track record. He hadn't been in the Senate for very long, and his opinions as a professor of constitutional law had never been made clear. People were being driven by optimism alone when they voted; they were disgusted with Bush. In my eyes it was the worst election in American history to date but it was historical to be sure, having the first African American man on the ticket.

When the dust cleared, Obama was the star of the show. He vowed almost instantly to close the detention facilities at Guantanamo Bay, Cuba. "Gitmo", as it's often called, housed the terror suspects. Some of those to be tried had confessed to involvement in the 9/11 attacks. The base came under scrutiny because of potential human rights violations. Arrests without warrants and failure to consider U.S. constitutional rights were investigated. Most agreed that wrong was done. The effect of Gitmo on the enemy was tremendous. Terrorists around the world knew that if caught, they would answer for their actions. Now with the stroke of a pen President Obama declared that the war on terrorism was over.

These actions were extremely satisfying to Americans on the home front. Generals smiled, shook hands, and posed for pictures, too timid to speak their minds. As the war on terror was recorded as a remnant of a paranoid time in our history, an IED was found on the road near our base in "friendly" Kuwait.

Meanwhile, civilians in Iraq were wounded when a bomb went off in Bagdad. In Afghanistan, too, the conflict continued. I guess that no one had told the insurgents that the war on terror was over. General David Petraeus had figured out a winning strategy in Iraq and was now running the show as perhaps the most universally respected general of my time. A surge was perfect for this type of war. Flood the country with troops, win the hearts and minds of the people, and success will follow.

A week to the day after arriving in Kuwait I fired my first shots outside the wire in a combat zone as a mass of camels scurried across the busy highway. Many of the troops had never seen a camel before. There were hundreds of them being herded by only a few men. The animals were large, dumb, and moved with little grace. It was rumored that for each camel accidentally killed our government had to pay a sum of ten thousand dollars to the owner. The herd was so spread out it was difficult to imagine any person could track them all. I imagined some oil-rich sheik somewhere living the good life while a few nomadic wanderers kept an eye on his camels, but more of an eye on the American soldiers.

We unmanned our vehicles and lined up to some stationary targets out in the middle of nowhere. I locked and loaded a magazine containing twenty rounds into my M4 assault rifle, turned on my red dot CCO scope, and nestled my rifle's buttstock into my shoulder. The Colt M4 is a beautiful weapon despite heavy scrutiny. It's a member of the M16 family. Many argue that the size of the round is too small, though I have never heard personally of anyone that survived a direct hit from the weapon as fired by a qualified U.S. soldier. It is lethal and it is simple to operate, even if its inner workings are complex compared to the AK-47. Our weapons were augmented by a SureFire tactical light mounted near the barrel for room to room clearing in poor visibility, a PEC 15 infrared laser targeting system for use with night vision goggles, the red dot CCO scope which makes killing as easy as point and click, and a collapsible buttstock.

My rifle is my friend and has been since before basic training. I killed my first animal, a box turtle, on my friend Ryan's grandmother's farm in South Carolina when I was very young. I shot it with a .22 at one hundred and fifty yards. It was a fluke that I hit my mark; there's no way in hell that I should have. From that time on, I guess I was a natural.

Before basic training I went to shooting ranges on a weekly basis with Mr. Scheid, a friend, mentor, and my town's former fire chief. During basic training I learned to love my rifle as an extension of myself. In Kuwait, I was able to ignore the camels. I stared through my scope and fired off my rounds. It was as natural as breathing. Afterwards, I smiled a great smile—the world was mine. I had fired my first rounds in a combat zone. It may have seemed lame to many, but I looked at it as a major milestone. It was an unpredictable time in the Middle East and here I stood ready to do my duty. It (the rifle) bestows on soldiers a divine power to eliminate opposition. Waiting to move forward on a base poised to accomplish that very aim, I anticipated the battles that could come in my empire's final drive into Iraq.

Mere days before the move north into Iraq, our battalion saw many of the deficiencies associated with our mobilization firsthand. Some observed that leaders spent too much time trying to make themselves look good by "checking the box" than actually assuring that our soldiers and equipment were combat effective. All of our Conex storage containers and vehicles were rail-headed back in Louisiana and were loaded onto the trains during a terrible rain storm. As a result, mold covered many of the vehicles. When we opened up the Conex boxes in Iraq there were some issues associated with mold and the damp conditions within the tomb like storage containers. One of Charlie Company's Strykers burst into a ball of flames while sitting at rest in a loading dock in Kuwait. It is rumored that this was the result of a wiring error. Only about fifty percent of the U.S.'s weapons were up, working, and certified for combat despite the fact that we were in a combat zone—a scary statistic. These were weapons like the fifty caliber machine gun. Most of these problems probably could have and should have been dealt with back in the U.S. Then again, it was Christmastime when we left and nobody likes to work on the holidays, even if your job is meant to improve soldiers' chances for survival later on. Now, in dust filled Kuwait, with plenty of time to think, it wasn't hard for soldiers' personal feelings of disdain to emerge. We truly were the red-headed stepchildren of our brigade.

The Marines at Camp Buehring were a sight to be seen. They were all members of one of the Marine Expeditionary Units, or MEUs. Fate had not been kind to these soldiers. Kuwait was now a transitional phase for them. Like us, they were trained for one main purpose: to engage and destroy the enemy. Having previously been on a ship, they likely hadn't seen much of the mountainous terrain of Afghanistan. Now they were in Kuwait, the gateway to the Iraq Theater of War. In Iraq, the changes in government, economics, and overall society meant that the only thing that was certain was that nothing was certain.

The Marines aren't any better than the Army. In fact, in many ways the Army provides superior equipment and training. The Marines we came across in Kuwait were much unlike how I envisioned their Fallujah tested brothers. They all dressed immaculately but their attitudes were just as crude as the regular Army grunt. Their body armor was coyote brown with no groin protection or neck guards. Their equipment seemed substandard compared to what we were using. Their Humvees didn't seem to be capable of providing much blast protection. However the Marine Corps does have something that the Army is decidedly lacking—pride in what they are. Some soldiers are proud as anything but all in all, the esprit de corps that Marines usually have is lost in the Army. We don't care as much about how our uniforms look or when our branch's birthday is, but we do care just as much about destroying the enemy. These Marines now stood envying the 56TH Stryker Brigade because, unlike them, we would be full filling our purpose. The Marines would not be entering Iraq. They were waiting for their boat. We were going to war and they were not. It reminded me of the Field Artillery Marines at Fort Sill and felt strange to be envied so openly by another branch.

# GUNS FORWARD

**A** **FEW DAYS LATER** we packed tightly onto buses and Humvees and moved to Camp Ali Al Salem, Kuwait. The Australians heavily occupied this camp. The Aussies' uniforms looked like they had just come out of a paint ball match. They were a colorful bunch who kept beer in their vehicles, just in case. Unfortunately, I wasn't at the camp for more than a few hours to observe them any further.

Each American solider carried a basic load of only thirty rounds of ammunition due to shortages. Congress was not supportive enough of us to make sure we had adequate ammo.

This was the night I would go to war. We crammed onto a packed U.S. Air Force C-130 aircraft. The flight itself took only an hour and a half. Soldiers lined on a net bench along both sides of the aircraft and huddled in a huge mass in the center of the plane's belly. The plane was nothing like a commercial aircraft. Instead it was loud with virtually no amenities. It did have a latrine but we were advised not to use it. We could see bare pipes and wires running all around us; it was like no scene I had ever seen, not even in a war movie. The takeoff and landing were the fastest and most exhilarating that I had ever experienced. It was like a PG-13 roller coaster. Any one tiny mishap could have upgraded it to an "R" rating.

Then I was in Bagdad, Iraq at what was once Saddam Hussein International Airport. When we landed, the giant hatch plopped open and we all struggled to stand and lug our heavy gear and weaponry around. Every time we moved I thought I would blow a disc in my back because of the sheer weight alone. Bagdad International still showed signs of distress from the many years of war. We expected to fly out of Bagdad the same night. Unfortunately, the post could not accommodate our transport to Taji that night. This meant I got to spend the day in Bagdad.

Palm trees and other vegetation surrounded us. Bagdad wasn't barren desert like where we had been in Kuwait. Instead there was a huge city. It was entirely built up with plentiful electricity, running water, and civilian access to the most modern technologies. We slept in tents with concrete bunkers lined with sandbags forming a solid perimeter around us (this was where we were to go in the event of a mortar attack.) We were only afforded a few hours of sleep before we had to return to the airport side of the post. We sat at the airport for hours on end as flights were bumped back time after time due to weather conditions and enemy threat levels.

It was in Bagdad that I encountered an elite group of black-uniformed Italian Army police. The Italians had built up quite a reputation for themselves. They wore riot gear and stormed into large crowds, pummeling all who stood before them. They followed their own version of the rules of engagement, throwing punches as part of their interrogations. It was even rumored that they ate like kings everywhere they went because they traveled with their own groups of Italian chefs. It was when I was distracted by trying to overhear what the Italians were conversing about that a loud voice came over a sound amplifier saying that a controlled detonation would occur in twenty minutes' time. By that time night had fallen. Moments later the sky revealed a huge red dome resembling a sunrise that lit up the whole sky. Every soldier among us stared in awe. Seconds later we heard the boom from the blast. I could tell from the time elapse from sight to sound that the blast was some ways away. Some members of our S-2 military intelligence group told me that the controlled detonation was a U.S. explosive ordinance disposal team whose target was either an IED or a captured weapons cache. It served as a reminder that the danger was real. Hours were spent on the cold flight line just thinking, wondering about all that was to come.

Our troops were shuttled to Taji via two methods. The first and predominant was the Chinook helicopter, which seated chalks (teams) of thirty soldiers. The second was the Marine Corps' Osprey, a vehicle infamous for crashing. The Osprey's wings cause it to rise upwards like a helicopter. The entire wing then spins on a rotation sending the vehicle soaring forward at high speeds. It looks like something out of a Terminator movie.

I loaded into one of the helicopters. It wasn't nearly as spacious as I had imagined it would be. I was roughly the fourteenth person out of thirty to board. We took off from the ground and turned off all of our interior running lights—we were running black—but you could still see everything that was going on because the city lights of Bagdad illuminated the skies. An Army aviation gunner manned a heavy machine gun and poised himself on the back loading ramp. The soldier was held in place and prevented from falling only by a thin strap. It was apparent that he was very good at his job. The ramp remained partially open for the entire flight. The hole exposed the weapon to the ground so that if need be we stood a chance of repelling an attack. As a result it was cold enough in the aircraft's cab that I could see my own breath. For some reason about mid-flight the pilot fired off two flares. I guessed that it was to let the Chinook that was behind us gauge its distance in order to avoid a collision but I really had no idea. It could have meant anything. It could have been a standard protocol or it could have meant that an Iran-built RPG narrowly missed us, its target. I will never know. None of the other 10 flights in our iteration reported firing off flares. All of this was new to me. I was experiencing it all for the fist time.

# AL TAJI

THE FLIGHT TO CAMP TAJI only lasted fifteen minutes. When we got there it was early morning and the sun had not yet risen. I went through the long and drawn out process of checking in to Camp Taji's personnel tracking system, then signed out a room key and hopped onto a congested coach bus. A few minutes later I was in POD 12, a trailer which was to be my temporary home. The trailer was much nicer than the tents that I had stayed in over the previous three months and because it was essentially a two-man room, it was far superior to the new Stryker barracks that I had stayed in back in Pennsylvania. It resembled a college dormitory in many ways. The room contained two small mattresses on steel frames, two wall lockers, two small tables, and two garbage receptacles.

That morning I missed sports history in the making. My hometown Pittsburgh Steelers had won their sixth Super Bowl championship, giving them more than any other team in NFL history. The win brought a glimmer of pride. I was many miles from my home in Pittsburgh but I still carried with me that hometown pride. There were lots of Steelers fans in my unit, a few Browns fans, and then there was the loveable SSG Dube—the lone Dallas Cowboys fan. Every Pennsylvania unit seemed to have one. Most of the guys were from Erie. Pittsburgh was my city, my home. It was my team. If my team back home could pull it off then perhaps my team in Iraq could too.

In Iraq I met the soldiers that I would be replacing, the 1-27TH Battalion, another Stryker Brigade Combat Team from the 25TH Infantry Division (Tropic Lightning). The division made its home in far off Hawaii. They had been in Iraq for fourteen long months when we arrived. Several of their soldiers had been killed in action. They were battle hardened and no joke, but they were tired. These soldiers were very similar to us in many ways. Like us, their brigade treated them poorly, chopping them up and dicing them into multiple platoons at different bases all over Iraq. Despite their hardships, they were great guys. I learned a lot from the 1-27TH. They were happy to teach, but eager to leave Iraq. They had done their time.

# NO CLASS 1

**A** **BIG PERK TO LIFE** at Al Taji was the Class 1 distribution center. Class 1 was in essence a huge warehouse packed with food and drinks. Units could go there to request anything from Gatorade to crab legs. Only a few months after the unit that we were replacing had left the country, my section was bestowed order forms to request anything that we might want. That didn't mean that we'd get everything that we asked for, however, if there was a surplus of goods, then we were in business. Some of my section's favorite picks included iced coffee, non-alcoholic beer, and Pop-tarts. Plenty of drama would come up over who got what.

Iraq was hell on my metabolism. I struggled to eat and work out right. In all honesty I probably didn't eat often enough and when I did it was usually all of the wrong things. It was nice to have access to the occasional goodies whether they were good for me or not.

A few times an older NCO in the battalion faced accusations for misusing Class 1 items for purposes of personal gain. To the best of my knowledge no concrete evidence was ever produced against him.

Everybody had their suspicions but the guy seemed to slip by safely, one step ahead of would be accusers. As far as the letter of the law went, all were innocent unless proven otherwise. There simply was no proof. Even if some goods were skimmed off the top, I'm not sure that I would have cared. It was an extreme hassle to physically go to the Class 1 distribution center. There were always long lines and a lot of bartering was required. I felt that the NCO was basically providing a service by picking things up for us much in the same way that a 7-Eleven provides convenience. It's more expensive than the local grocery store but it's easier. The way I viewed it, anything extra was much better than nothing at all.

No one in my small section found room to complain about such petty things when we were in a place where there was so much more to worry about. Almost daily I'd hear tales of violence in some corner of Iraq. Sure, there were worse places to be than Al Taji or Istaqlal—the posts that I was at—but there was no safe haven for U.S. servicemen overseas in that day and age.

Only a few weeks after arriving in Iraq our battalion commander, LTC Flanegan, was in a convoy with a bunch of guys from the 1-27TH Infantry. Their battalion commander, LTC Flip Wilson, was a fun loving guy. The 1-27TH carried the same relaxed attitude that you would think people who lived in paradise (in their cases, Hawaii) might have. He called people "brah" and made hand gestures. He was one cool cat. Both LTC Flanegan and LTC Wilson were experienced and on the verge of major promotions. They had literal teams of soldiers called personal security detachments (PSDs) that were responsible for their protection. Every time we left the wire there was a human shield built up around the commander. While in transit these shields weren't needed; we used the Strykers. The convoy was hit by an improvised explosive device. A charge of molten metal ripped through one of the Strykers in a grand explosion. LTC Flanegan led us as our battalion commander. He also led our battalion in being its first member to experience combat during our deployment. With the IED blast, Flanegan became a combat infantryman. All soldiers involved in that action survived the day.

# ISTAQLAL

**W**HEN I WASN'T AT TAJI I was at Istaqlal. Istaqlal was a worthless piece of land that provided allied forces with an overwatch of Sadr City. Sadr City wasn't friendly. The people there hated us and had close ties to al-Qaeda in Iraq. When we drove through the town, little children would throw rocks at us and scream in Arabic. We didn't have a clue what they were saying. We didn't really want to be there and the people clearly didn't want us there either. Had it been up to us it would have been a short tour of duty.

Istaqlal was a Joint Service Station (JSS), which meant we shared it with the Iraqi Army. The small post emitted a unique smell that was far from pleasant. The living areas had beds but as I was only there in short bursts I was given a folding canvas cot. I didn't mind. I only had to be there a few days at a time where other soldiers spent the majority of their deployment there. There were patrols out of the JSS nearly every day, unless a dust storm prevented them from happening.

Serving in such close proximity to Sadr City earned me a little more respect when I returned to Taji. People had heard of Sadr City. If you asked a college student of the time where the fighting was going on in Iraq they would have replied with: Baghdad, Fallujah, or Sadr City. Moqtada al Sadr's Mahdi militia was no joke. They were the lone hold-outs in our region to the newly implemented Iraqi regime. In a way they were like the Wolverines in the 1980s cult classic film *Red Dawn,* only this time we were the foreign invaders. The Mahdi militiamen were surprisingly well trained, especially in explosive ordinance. Their greatest strength was that they could easily implant their members into the Iraq Army or National Police. It was impossible to gauge the level of allegiance of our Iraq allies.

We had a strong support system at Istaqlal. We were Operational Control (OPCON) for the 56TH Brigade because the JSS was out of their scope of practice. OPCON is a term that's used when elements of a unit are assigned to another unit in order to make them more effective in carrying out their mission. We were attached to a parachute infantry regiment (PIR) of the Third Brigade, 82nd Airborne Division. The 82nd guys were pure professionals—hard chargers that jumped out of airplanes on a regular basis. They were on the ball and all of them were airborne qualified. Because my team wasn't normally an airborne regiment, we were called "leg" soldiers. In airborne units only soldiers who jump tuck their dress pants into their boots. Non-jumpers don't tuck in their pants and thus have strait legs, hence the name "leg soldiers", which can be used both as an insult and as a term of endearment. Most of the paratroopers had multiple combat infantry engagements. Originally I had thought that their level of competence would make them look at our guys and treat them poorly. The opposite was true. They loved us.

In the earlier days of the deployment the 56TH Brigade had said that we weren't allowed to wear combat patches until six months had elapsed. The 82nd guys said that this was dangerous. Their Sergeant Major handed out 82nd Airborne patches for us to wear. "The enemy knows what a combat patch means," said the Sergeant Major. "Don't give them a reason to test you." The first people that I actually saw wearing the patches in country were 1LT Whitney and SSG Dube—two of our best. Being a part of the 82nd taught me how the military should be. No one judged you on anything other than how you performed. They valued the trigger pullers. Back in Pittsburgh, when I had been in the support battalion, the opposite was true: it was physical fitness, appearance, and marksmanship they valued, but they treated the actual trigger pullers like shit.

The trigger pullers are the only ones that make a proven difference in combat but the trigger pullers weren't the ones that were re-enlisting because they were so undervalued by the organization. There's a huge difference between those that have been mortared and those that are real trigger pullers. I was never an infantrymen but I started to look at myself as a trigger puller because that's how the men of the 82nd treated me. They valued me. I knew that I could act under fire and kill the enemy if need be but I also knew that there were many that could not.

With our Stryker crews the 82nd kept Sadr City under their thumbs. The Mahdi militia didn't want to rumble with us because they knew that if they did it would be a useless sacrifice. I was appreciative to have such feared and respected mentors. Later, when the 1st Cavalry Division replaced us at Istaqlal, the militia went into test mode again. The unit from the 1st Cavalry had disrespected the local populace, practiced marksmanship on wild dogs and their puppies, and kicked in some of the wrong doors. It was like night and day for the local Iraqis who begged us to stay and requested that the 1st Cavalry go away.

# ANOTHER NEW FACE

I WAS WELL INTO MY overseas tour when I met SGT Sullivan. He came to us from the inactive ready reserve. He had already done a tour in Iraq and was enjoying a successful civilian career at a Fortune 500 company in Florida when Uncle Sam called upon him again. Before he knew it he was back in the Army. Like me, he held a degree in history. He also had many similar interests such as writing letters to prominent figureheads (During my time in Iraq I was pleased to receive both a written reply as well as an autographed photograph from Arnold Schwarzenegger, bodybuilding legend, star of the silver screen, and Governor of the State of California.)

Sullivan could probably be described as a somewhat nerdy black kid and we often poked fun at his blatantly Irish last name. On his very first day with us I gave him my extra keystone combat patch so he could wear it and feel more like one of us. Since that moment he and I got along together quite well. Of course there were occasionally arguments that came up but it was that way with everyone. He had more knowledge about mail operations than I did and he was always quick to share his knowledge freely with me. We worked together daily for roughly a month before he was called away to work on a military audio/visual photography team.

Throughout the course of the year the S-1 section would be tapped of its personnel and resources to create AV teams or similar ventures. Pearson and McDonald also spent time on the AV team. It felt to us as if our command was assuming that my shop simply didn't have anything better to do when in reality we had more than most others on our plate. With more guys gone my workload nearly tripled.

As AV team members, my compatriots didn't have it easy either. They went on missions multiple times a week, from foot patrols, to mounted convoys and helicopter air assaults. They took countless pictures and wrote hundreds of pages while reporting on our brigade's activities. Pearson would sometimes get discouraged, feeling like he was being used inappropriately. Journalism was an actual military occupation though, that had its own advanced training. Yet as equipment and human resource specialists, none of us were entirely proficient in it. On paper, Sullivan was good for the job. He already hosted a successful online blog about his "involuntary recall". I don't think anyone actually liked it.

I personally would get extra duties or details all the time. It wouldn't necessarily be helping out the AV team, but duties with the S-4 section and battalion supply became my norm. I was always doing something. I thanked God for helping me develop the time management skills that I had over the past years. Still, every night we'd make time to play poker or just sit around for a few minutes to complain and laugh to each other about the day's events.

I would spend at least three days out of each week on the road, delivering mail and dealing with IEDs and the occasional sporadic small arms rifle fire—never anything worth writing home about. I volunteered to stand in as a gunner on the convoys as often as I could. The warm dusty breeze felt on the convoys, seeing the local people and children come to the side of the road to watch us, watching for trash or debris that could potentially be an IED—I was doing the deed.

# TEMPLAR ARMY

**S**INCE I WAS A CHILD I always dreamt of being a Freemason. Growing up I had seen their monuments throughout Pennsylvania. I'd witnessed their logos on buildings and money, and I'd read the books and watched the movies. The opportunity to join the Mason ranks finally came in Iraq when one of their members asked me if I'd be willing to go through an entry process. I eagerly agreed but in truth I knew very little about the Masonic lodges. Much of what I thought I knew turned out to be false. At first, many of the questions I had for the members got brushed aside with responses like, "It's not a secret society, it's a society with secrets" or "You'll know when your light shines through." I soon discovered much more practical information.

The Masons were transplanted to the New World along with the thirteen colonies. Since that time, American Freemasonry evolved into something completely different than its European counterparts, though the two do share common origins. No matter where you are in the world you can find Masons, but not all of the men in the global arena will hold the same principles, knowledge, or beliefs.

In the United States the Masons have distinguished themselves as masters of philanthropy, running hospitals that save lives and fighting for worthy causes.

Wearing a Masonic ring could mean the difference between getting a promotion and getting laid off. In the Army, the former seemed to be the case. American Masons were divided into two groups: the Free and Accepted and the Prince Hall Masons. The Prince Hall Masons were somewhat of an offshoot spawned from racial and social tensions. As far as I could tell there was far more diversity in the latter. It was the Prince Hall Masons that invited me to become a brother.

I went through long ceremonies and completed the 1st Degree before I started to have doubts about not only my ability to split my time between the Freemasons and the military, but also the very system that I was joining. Being a Mason took a lot of time and dedication that, while maybe plentiful back in the States, was hard to come by in Iraq. I didn't feel right coming up with excuses and lies because I couldn't be honest with my platoon sergeant about where I was going. It was hard to disappear for hours on end when it was important for people to know where I was at all times. I didn't like the idea of showing other Masons so much preferential treatment when we were all soldiers deployed in a combat zone. I loved all of my brother soldiers. Finally there were religious implications. Things were said that I didn't agree with. As a Mason you didn't have to believe in God per say, but you did have to believe in a supreme being, even if it was a deity like Zeus or Satan. At the same time I was actually told that the King James Bible was the "only correct version" of that text. As a Catholic, some of this was hard to swallow. I made up my mind that at that point in my life, joining the Freemasons wasn't in line with my other beliefs.

I met with one of the only Catholic priest in Iraq, Father Kozen. He told me that for one reason or another the Catholic Church had forbade membership in the Masons but that he thought that might change soon and I would be better served seeking council from my home diocese. Some help, huh? I contacted a priest in Pittsburgh who told me that it was against Canon Law to be a Mason. The Masons were set up like a religion, and membership was set up so that it barred Catholics from Communion. All this made the choice even easier; I left the Masons prior to becoming a full member.

A few of their members continued to harass me over the next few weeks but by and large most of them dealt with me with class. I wasn't the only one to walk away. Several other soldiers did the same. I have nothing but respect for many of the things that Masons do to contribute to society. Looking back at it, I did already learn the concept of social brotherhood in a fraternal organization from being a Delta Sigma alum. I don't judge the Freemasons and I hoped that most of them would continue to see me as a friend. I guess it's just not for everyone.

# SPLITTING UP THE TEAM: ISTAQLAL, HOR AL BASH, WAR EAGLE, AL TAJI

**A**L TAJI WASN'T A BASE that the coalition constructed as a mere response to the initial invasion in 2003. In another life the base served as the home for Saddam Hussein's armored tank corp. It was literally the Iraqi version of our Fort Knox. It was there that Iraq housed a multitude of tanks, artillery pieces, and weaponry. Much of this hardware was produced in the Soviet Union, however German, French, and American weaponry was also used over the years.

While he was in power Hussein boasted one of the largest military forces in the world. He used his soldiers and equipment to instill a rough balance throughout the Middle East. He scared the living shit out of Iran, his neighbor to the east. Whether or not Hussein had actually developed a successful chemical weapons program is highly debated even today. Most in the military believed that there were chemical weapons and that many of them were smuggled into Syria. We do know that in the past the country had both possessed and utilized SCUD missiles against various targets. In the Gulf War however, his missiles, tanks, and aircraft proved no match for American firepower.

In 1991 Al Taji was the center for Hussein's armor corp and remained so until 2003 when it was easily taken by American and British forces. While I was there the base was split in half: an Iraqi side and an American side. The American side looked much like any other allied post. There, the American flag flew freely and American soldiers outnumbered all others. The only thing that distinguished this base from any base in the southwestern United States was the bone yard. After we invaded, all of the old armored vehicles stayed. Al Taji was under new management. Not only could you see Abrams, Strykers, and Bradleys but you could also see the rusting shells of tanks and aircraft that used to make up a premier Middle Eastern army. Soldiers would take their pictures with the old tanks and spray paint personalized messages onto them. They then sent the photos home as mementoes for loved ones. I prided myself on shipping home old-style Iraqi flags, insignia, dinar bank notes, captured enemy bayonets, and other war trophies as mementoes.

Getting around was often difficult as we had no personal transportation to get from one end of the post to the other. I found it humorous when a group of Army engineers found an original solution to this transportation problem. They took one of the old Russian armored transports, plugged the barrel, and repaired it so that it functioned normally. The mini-tank still had a triangle in a circle—a logo of the old Iraqi Army—painted on its fore and aft. It became a personal vehicle to the engineers who used it to go to the chow hall, the gym, or the bootleg movie store. Not many people knew what to make of the tiny, armored, turtle-like car. Eventually it must have caught the eye of either the military police or some other high-ranking official. Perhaps it just stopped running one day. Either way, I didn't see it scooting around more than three times throughout the duration of my own tour of duty.

# THE BAGHDAD MASSACRE

I**N MAY WE WERE ALL** very disheartened to receive word of murders in nearby Baghdad. The violence targeted American troops. What made this story so different from traditional ones is that the perpetrator was also an American serviceman—a sergeant seeking counseling at a combat stress clinic at Camp Liberty in Baghdad. People often underestimate just how stressful an overseas tour can be. You always had to be on your toes. You had to be alert 24/7 even when you were on a major FOB. Once you left the bases things were even more elevated. It was a scary place and some guys had to do terrible things. Afterwards, they were left to deal with what they had seen alone.

Earlier in the day on May 11, 2009 the sergeant had visited the clinic where he was disarmed. Everybody in Iraq carried a weapon. The sergeant stole weapons from a supply depot and returned later and killed five of his fellow American soldiers. It was terrible, almost more so because it happened at a location minutes away from Baghdad International Airport, which was at the time considered to be one of the safer locations in the country.

My heart went out to the families of those murdered. I also felt for the guy that pulled the trigger. He obviously needed help. The U.S. military does a much better job taking care of its soldiers' medical needs than any other military organization I have ever interfaced with, however the medical/physical side and the mental side of things are not treated equally. The U.S. is improving but even today lacks in the diagnosis and care of returning war veterans with traumatic brain injuries or combat stress. In large, these men are neglected and this needs to change in the future.

We all looked at the incident with weary eyes. Stay alert, stay alive. My goal wasn't to kill the enemy. My goal was just to get home in one piece. Some of my brothers wouldn't be going home. I hope that the people in the United States recognize what we went through. We did it all for them. I found myself sad and unhappy often, but I knew that I was fortunate to be alive. The saddest thing about being blessed is that it often feels as if you are cursed.

# THE IRAQI SIDE

S TEPPING FOOT ONTO the Iraq Army side of Al Taji was something like being an astronaut and taking those first steps onto a distant world. It might as well have been an old episode of *Star Trek*. There was a different culture there, a different language, different clothing, different religion, different weapons and different values. I didn't have to board a futuristic spacecraft to get this experience. It was all at my fingertips right there in Iraq. The entry point to the Iraq side of the post was manned lightly by civilian contractors and Ugandans on the American side and entirely unmanned on the Iraqi side. I had the benefit of a great many trips to the Iraqi side of the post, most of which were near the end of my own tour of duty.

The first time I was there I was nervous. It was nighttime and many of the buildings were bombed remnants from the initial 2003 invasion. There were sporadic packs of stray dogs running all around us. Most of my time on their side of the tracks was spent at an Army barracks that housed the IA Army and National Police, of which my own battalion was tasked with assisting. There I was a guest of the officer corps, which was different from ours to say the least. All of their officers sported bare feet rather than boots when hanging out in the garrison. They lived six persons to a small room. The major benefit to their room was that they had an air conditioning unit. The AC had uneven holes of concrete sticking out from the structure because the building had no windows naturally built into it. Therefore, to install the AC units the Iraqi people took sledgehammers and bashed into the concrete slab, creating a place to house the machines. The result was not visually appealing at all. It was like trying to fit a square into a smaller circular hole.

The officers were very young. I met the S1 equivalent to myself, an Iraqi captain who was ever so pleased to have gotten a printer for his circa-1992 computer. The soldiers' uniforms were all different patterns and colors. As a point of fact they were not very uniform at all. Their weapon of choice was the Soviet made AK-47 machine rifle. This was the same weapon that the enemy was using in most small arms fire encounters that we saw throughout the Middle East. The Iraqi Army officers were friendly, in fact overly so. I questioned the sexual orientation of a few of them. They were quick to offer the traditional chai tea and cigarettes, but even quicker to accept whatever we would give them, typically what was left from the onslaught of care packages our guys would receive from our supporters back home.

Some of our soldiers ordered appliances and items such as refrigerators, bicycles, and writing supplies from websites such as Wal-Mart, then sold that same merchandise at a huge premium markup to the Iraqi soldiers and the populace that typically paid cash in American dollars, not dinars. It always felt to me like their guys consistently had more money than ours did to buy comfort items. Some of my fellow Americans grew to feel so comfortable with our foreign friends that they would leave their weapons in the backs of their vehicles and walk around among the Iraqi populace completely unprotected, a practice that always made me feel completely vulnerable and uncomfortable. I should not have enjoyed going over to the Iraqi side of the post as much as I did, but I think the unorganized military rabble that existed there provided me a small adrenaline boost.

# THE MARKETS: THE IRAQ ARMY SIDE

**T**HE MOST ENTERTAINING part of the Iraqi Army side of the base was, to me, the marketplace. The merchant center was flooded with Iraqi civilians. There were sometimes so many of them that it became nerve wracking to say the least. The simple truth was that, should those people have become hostile, there would be little if anything that we could have done to fight back before meeting our own untimely demise. One personal side effect of the war was a strong dislike of being in crowds.

The market was composed of tiny shops, some actual buildings and others made of sheets and blankets. There was a bakery that sold unleavened flat bread. For a huge stack of the bread the cost was around five dollars American. There was a uniform repair shop where those that could afford to could purchase insignia and other patches as well as uniform accessories. There was a diner that served all sorts of Middle Eastern dishes, of course at an elevated price for Americans. The icing on the cake was the soft-serve frozen yogurt vendor, though that's not what people typically envision when they think of a combat tour in Iraq.

I actually got really sick for about four weeks because I made the potentially grave error of eating their food. Other countries do not maintain same sanitary standards that we do in the United States. The majority of our Iraq counterparts had decent lodgings, but despite that slept outside on the ground during the summer months. I was told that this was not because it was cooler outside but rather because the barracks were virtually a breeding ground for mosquitoes and other disease-carrying insects. Very few of their people had vehicles and those that did were either sheiks or high-ranking officials. As a result of this there were lots of people walking alongside the dirt winding roads, many were holding up a thumb, the universal symbol for the hitchhiker. This occurred at all hours of the day and night.

The one thing that I respected the most about people of Iraq is the same thing that many feared—their devotion to their religious ideologies and spiritual well being. I've not seen religious Westerners in such high quantities anywhere in all of my travels. Five times a day, though, these people were on their knees praying. They weren't just reciting words aloud; they all knew without a shadow of doubt the truth in their words and they believed that Allah was out there and still looking after his people. Can you imagine having your whole world ripped away, living in a war-torn society and still maintaining such a perfect confidence in God? This happens on a mass scale every day in Iraq and is one aspect that I respected the hell of.

Some people blame religion and religious differences for strife. Just as sure as Christianity has been manipulated to accomplish horrible things in human history, so have other world religions. Being a Catholic college student at a private Lutheran school, I once had to debate the Catholic Church's role in the Crusades, the Inquisition, and even the Holocaust. All were terrible events at least partially inspired by religion and there are countless other examples of religious-based atrocities that have appeared throughout the ages. I am still proud of my religious beliefs, traditions, and values because, let's face it, they made me the man that I am today. I'm also very compassionate towards other religions. I have to say I thought it was awesome that the people of the Middle East cared so very much about their own religion. They weren't anything like us and at the same time, they were us. The differences that did exist were largely material.

When I did go on "house-to-house" missions on foot with the infantry platoon, though dangerous, it was not what I had expected. I had felt that the action would resemble something out of *Black Hawk Down*, kicking in the door and rushing the building, rounding up prisoners and enforcing our will. I served during a period of reconstruction though. We started our door-to-door searches much more politely by simply knocking on the door and waiting for the people who lived there to answer. In retrospect this was not wise, and a poor decision. The rules of engagement were so strict that our platoon leaders always had to exercise extreme caution.

I got letters in the mail all the time. Some were from family, some from friends, and some from total strangers. An interesting question that I was once asked was presented to me in a letter by students at a high school just miles out of Pittsburgh, Pennsylvania. I was asked as a soldier whether or not I believed we were winning or losing the wars, which were occurring in both Afghanistan and Iraq and were offshoots of the Global War on Terrorism. For me that seemed a very difficult question to answer and I think it depends entirely on how you defined a win at the time. In Iraq we had learned many lessons, which had given our military invaluable experience; however the death tolls, civilian and military, as well as the financial cost of the war seemed to increase dramatically over time. In my opinion, both of these outcomes are completely unacceptable.

In Afghanistan violence escalated as American soldiers were being outnumbered by al-Qaeda fighters, something that should never have been allowed to happen. To make matters worse, the opium traders, who were armed drug runners, fit the exact description of the enemy. With drugs being huge sources of income for that country, we had to make it clear time and again that Afghanistan, at least publicly, was not a front in the war on drugs. We weren't officially at war to dissolve the Afghan narcotics trade, and yet in the fog of war, skirmishes were often breaking out between allied coalition forces and the drug runners. These things happened in Iraq too as a new mafia crime class rose to power. The most effective strategy in the allied arsenal, the "surge" of troops, was being contested and resisted at every pass. The government denies this to this day but I believe that the real reason for our ongoing presence in Iraq and Afghanistan is actually to maintain a tactical overwatch of the country of Iran. If this is the case, then we have most certainly won already; we have Iran completely surrounded.

A major problem was that no one was releasing a clear-cut objective for the Iraq War or operations in OEF. When I was deployed there was much talk of pullouts and pullbacks, but when it was all over nothing had changed. As we were saying that we were going to pull out we were simultaneously building up at bases such as Al Taji with construction projects worth millions, if not billions, of dollars. What we were saying as a country publicly and what we were doing as country privately conflicted greatly. Why were we there? This question has never been answered with clarity. Was it to catch and slay Bin Laden? Everyone knew that Bin Laden was safe in either Saudi Arabia or Pakistan, and not a soul felt there was an actual possibility that he was in Afghanistan. Saddam Hussein was long gone and thus was no longer a threat.

There were new threats. Insurgency and terrorism were both evolving at a rapid pace. It felt like we were impacting every world event that would follow for the next hundred years or longer. There were new threats, threats that were far worse, but our guidance for addressing them was ill defined.

I think that you'll discover that if this student asked his question with a specific definition of the word "win" in mind, he might have found that it would be simple for anyone to answer the question on whether or not we were winning in Iraq and Afghanistan. We had been winning the vast majority of our combat engagements with the enemy, however I could say the same thing about the battles of the Vietnam or the Spanish American War. Does anyone really win in Manifest Destiny? The truth of the matter is that it's all a matter of basic human opinion. Wherever your original opinion lies is what you're going to lean towards when it comes to deciding the righteousness of the Global War on Terror Whether it's right or wrong is not for me to say. The next generation will make up its mind on whether or not my generation was successful. Such is history. Every generation must hope that the next will do the right things. All you can ever really do is your best.

A lot would change over the next few years and no one was exactly positive what was going to happen. That's how it's always been. There has always been darkness. It is a matter of choice to focus on the light, no matter how dim it might seem. It is always wise to hold an open-minded disposition and hopefully we can do the right thing because ultimately what America should be all about is doing the right things in the face of tyranny. As far as my personal service in Operation Iraqi Freedom I can say that I feel that I did the right thing. Emotionally I won, and I lost. I would forever be both blessed and tormented by what I endured. Life has storms, both literally and figuratively. Sandstorms were a part of life. The dust took visibility down to zero.

Helicopters could not fly and convoys could not roll. The only ones out during long dust storms were the insurgents who knew that they could easily bury roadside bombs in a no-risk scenario. For all of our technology, the storms rendered our infantry battalion useless in the harsh weather. Nature provided a reality check for us. Even with all of our power there was nothing that could be done to beat the laws of nature and the laws of God. In this realization is a timeless lesson about how we should perceive our own importance. When you went outside in one of these storms, even if only for a moment, you were caked with dust. It burned the eyes and made the throat sore. It was a common part of life in Iraq and a constant reminder of how frail we really were. From dust we all came and to dust we will all one-day return.

# SWEET SLOW PUMP

EVEN WHEN A "DAY-OFF" scheduling protocol was established I quickly discovered that running a unit mailroom wouldn't allow me to miss work very often. The mail would come in and require an armed escort every day whether I liked it or not. When my day off came around I would typically sleep in until roughly eight in the morning, then get dressed and mosey down to the tactical operations center. Even the privilege of being able to sleep in once a week eventually disappeared completely. I'm not sure that anyone else in the battalion really understood just how difficult it was to keep daily mail operations running smoothly and efficiently. Random inspections occurred all too often. Usually I did an exceptional job. Things had to be perfectly organized to standard and I really didn't have any supervision at all. I ran the whole thing how I wanted to and basically did whatever I wanted to as long as regulations were followed.

It wasn't entirely uncommon for me to lock up shop and hang out with the company guys from HHC. As long as complaints were kept at a minimum, which they were, I had job security. Throughout the whole year I only recorded four complaints and paperwork proved that they weren't directly my fault. Some packages went missing or ended up in strange places. Sometimes guys would call me every name in the book saying that their wives had sent them things, only to get the object sent registered months later. If you've ever had issues with the postal service in the United States, which many people have, then it's not surprising that some of those issues translate over to the Army postal system abroad.

The downside to all the work was that I often missed out on extra-curricular MWR events and activities. These activities were designed to relieve stress. A sergeant by the name of Kris Kersey and myself had planned on doing a Saturday Night Live Chippendales skit for a talent show with me playing the Chris Farley character. I had to work. There was a combative mixed martial arts tournament that I wanted to take part in. I had to work. There was even a chance to run a half marathon through Iraq. Two of the guys in my section got to run it and were out for several days after because of the heat. They weren't happy about the pain but at least they got to try it. I wanted to but again, I had to work. I always felt like it was a bad deal but I knew in my heart that it could be much worse and that part of being a man is playing the cards one is dealt.

Needless to say I didn't have too many outlets to vent my frustrations. I loved it when someone would play a funny prank or I'd see a funny drawing of our command sergeant major done with sharpie markers on the wall in the restroom. Things like that helped to break up long days and nights. One thing that helped me to cool down was my band. Some people might think I'm joking but I was the lead singer of a band.

*Rock Band* was a video game that was played on the Xbox 360, the premier gaming system at the time. The USO had mailed us one, complete with games. The entire set up included a guitar, drum sticks, and a microphone. It was a modern form of karaoke and we were blessed enough to have it at our base. SPC Crance and SGT Heintzel came up to me one day and said, "We need a singer." This confused me because prior to that I hadn't sung in front of anyone in the brigade and had also never played the game before. Still, I was bored so I eagerly accepted and became the lead singer of Sweet Pump.

For some reason I could never remember the band's name. I would always mess up during introductions and call us Slow Pump. And so Sweet Slow Pump was born. Crance was on the guitar. Heintzle rocked out on the drums. I took the lead microphone. Not the strongest singer, I made up for my vocal deficiencies by being colorful, vibrant, and injecting short strands of profanity wherever possible.

We entertained a lot of troops and probably disgusted a few. I started singing more. I entertained my neighbors SFC Anderson and SFC Black. It made people laugh and was absolutely worthwhile. Occasionally we still see each other in what we call "reunion tours". The experience definitely helped me to break out of my shell a bit.

Another way that I passed time during lulls in action was to write poetry. I would often have rap battles with Damyan Graves, an infantry captain and police officer. I did fairly well in my amateur rap career until my grandmother gave everyone plentiful ammunition to use against me. Grandma had misunderstood a letter that I had written home in which I said my uniform was so dirty after one mission that I threw away every piece of it, even my underwear. Grandma reacted to this by writing the local paper in Pittsburgh, explaining to them that the Army did not issue underwear to soldiers and that there was a shortage. The result of this was pallets upon pallets of underwear being sent to me in the mail. It got to be enough of an issue that my battalion commander addressed it with me. There were boxers, briefs, and tiger striped thongs. It was ridiculous. We gave most of it to the Iraqis. God only knows what they did with it. I didn't win any rap battles after that… there were just too many things that rhymed with "Hanes" and "Fruit of the Loom".

# HOR AL BASH

THE NAME HOR AL BASH wouldn't mean a thing to those that didn't serve there. The convoy there from Al Taji lasted only an hour, if that. On one mission, we were supposed to escort a group of engineers and their equipment to a village where they would drill a well that could provide fresh water to the community. We were to drive them there, drop them off, and return to the JSS. About half of the way there our vehicle took small arms fire, and a couple of pings and snaps slapped against our armored vehicle. The lead gunner, a private first class, was afraid to shoot back. We were all scared. I took his place on the turret and laid a few suppressive rounds into a building near the road. I thought that's where the shots came from. I was the only one shooting, and only popped off one, maybe two rounds. Lost in the moment, I fired until my Captain physically reached up from the passenger seat of the hummer and grabbed me, screaming for me to cease-fire. I fell from the gun exhausted, more stressed than actually tired. My hands were shaking with a nervous twitch. A pool of black fluid was forming at the doorstep of the building that I had opened up on. It could have been oil, or blood, spilled so quickly that it hadn't had a chance to oxidize into the familiar red. I had met my mark, but what had I done? Was I now a killer? In my head I had first tried to explain to myself that the blood was in reality something like oil, but I didn't know. Eventually I convinced myself that I maintained my innocence. No one was found dead or injured, or in the area at all. We kept driving.

Another team later found rifles, grenades, and bomb making equipment in that very shack. Apparently I was justified. What bothered me the most about the situation was that it really didn't bother me at all afterwards. It was easy. I hadn't really done anything at all. I was also surprised by the reaction of my peers. No one asked me if I was all right or how I felt. Instead everyone wanted to high five me and pat me on the back. The 82nd guys loved that I did SOMETHING. And back in my own company, it was as if nothing had even happened at all; no one mentioned it. I was a person that would act, that was all that my fellow soldiers needed to know.

I still think about that event sometimes. Every ounce of my moral intuition is against killing, but I wanted to be a soldier and soldiers kill. I have always been a spiritual person and I have found strong comfort in my religion. I often wonder how my God will judge me for the actions that I have made in this world. I hope that my God is an understanding one, as I believe he is. I prayed the rosary for two hours that night, and then went to sleep.

# BATMAN

**A**N INHERENT PART OF combat service in a time such as the one in which we were serving was boredom. There are a lot of ways in which troops deal with boredom; most of the more memorable ways are innocent and humor-based. One story that I always liked to tell about my time in Iraq is the story of one soldier and a Batman costume.

We were obviously very far from our homes and people looked for ways to pass the time and ease tensions. One soldier accomplished this by going onto a website and ordering himself a replica of a movie-quality Batman costume. This costume was complete with utility belt and phony muscles. He donned this costume, grabbed his rifle, and took a short tour of our FOB. Things went crazy as the masked marauder brought humor and enjoyment to all he encountered. Soon thereafter another soldier was seen dressed as the Joker.

Of course that all changed when two military police officers took a special interest and asked the young soldier for his identification card. "Batman never reveals his true identity," was the soldier's reply. This angered the police who quickly learned that this soldier was one of ours. They took him before the battalion commander, Colonel Flanagan. At first the colonel didn't seem very amused. He dismissed the military policemen and focused his attention on Batman. "Take off your mask", he said. The soldier took off his mask. The colonel replied, "That's funny, you don't look like Batman, you look much more like Bruce Wayne." The soldier received a light slap on the wrist but given the stressful environment he was spared UCMJ legal actions against him. Most of my fellow S-1 clerks weren't quite sure how to take this story. Most of them, like me, opted to take it with a laugh.

Another interesting story involved the battalion we replaced, the Wolf Hounds. While on a long convoy one of their young enlisted members became angry at how leadership was handling things. They were outside the wire in full battle rattle gear and the NCO in charge and the soldier got into a tiff. The soldier was enraged. The NCO then said to the soldier, "If you don't like how I'm running the show then hand off your weapon and walk back to base." Of course, the leader was being sarcastic. To walk back to base would've been an inconvenience and a suicide mission. The soldier, hailing from the 25TH Infantry Division, turned in his weapon by placing it inside the Stryker. He then began the long walk to Al Taji. On the way he found and picked up an AK-47 rifle just in case he would need it for personal defense.

When he got close to Taji the gate guards didn't know what to make of him. They had never seen a single U.S. service member armed as such and walking towards such a heavily guarded coalition checkpoint. After taking his weapon from him and verifying his identity he was released into the custody of the military police brigade. They in turn, initiated a full investigation. By all accounts, the soldier's actions were as "bad ass" and "hardcore" as it got. Very few people would attempt such a walk alone and in 130 plus degree weather. Under normal circumstances the soldier would've at the very least underwent a serious battery of strenuous mental evaluations. Because of what the NCO had said to the soldier, the soldier got off scot-free The event was actually interpreted as being an order. The soldier expressed that he felt he had been ordered to walk back to the post. The soldier was not rewarded nor was he punished.

A result of the training and the personal experiences that we each were having in the country was an extremely paranoid mindset. Every civilian could be a potential enemy. Every piece of trash alongside the highway could be a roadside bomb. We were alert and we were ready. Of course this changed the longer we were in country. We didn't want it to, but we relaxed nonetheless as do all soldiers in a similar position. The more time we were there, the more accustomed we became to the hell that was all around us. Things became lax. There was many times where what would have been funny (in a dark humor sort of way) became typical. One story that I like to share revolves around my good friend Christopher Crance. On paper Chris would be your typical Army soldier. A recent high school graduate, he decided to follow in his father's footsteps and enlist in the Army as an infantryman. In the Army he found a niche. He was a well-liked Stryker crewman and was anything but typical. You'd be hard pressed to find anyone that disliked him.

Despite having heavily armored vehicles, some platoon leaders preferred to have their soldiers dismount and walk on patrols. Many saw walking as being safer than riding. On one such patrol Chris gazed across an open field and noticed a dark figure in the distance. On top of the figure's head was a piece of cloth with a red and white checkered pattern design, a signal that the man had made the religious pilgrimage known to us as the "Haj". What was most scary about this figure was that his shape clearly changed around the waist area. He was holding something. A deep squint revealed the object as being an AK-47 rifle. Its shape and exaggerated long magazine made the weapon easy to pick out of a crowd and is the same type of weapon utilized by the enemy in various small arms confrontations around the world.

At that point Chris got excited. He made sure that his own rifle was locked and loaded. He was ready to go. Then he ran to an NCO from the 25TH division and informed him of what he had observed. In doing this Chris might have protected his men from a potential ambush and given them additional time to clear the open area and attempt to find some natural form of cover or concealment. The training had worked! Crance was surprised when the NCO didn't react. "It's okay kid, that's just a herder. He's got a right to protect his flock." There were indeed a few animals in the immediate area. The man was given no additional attention. He was not searched. The group continued on mission.

Was the NCO wrong? I would say so! It made little sense to ignore potential threats, even if doing so took more time. If given the choice between arriving on schedule versus arriving alive, an American soldier should always choose life, for all of his men.

There are all types of lessons that can be learned from this story. No soldiers died that day, however a lower precedent for security had been passed on from an experienced battalion to an inexperienced one. We were starting to look the other way rather than take action, especially when it got closer to the time that we would be going home ourselves. It was generally understood that the risk just wasn't worth it. The juice wasn't worth the squeeze. Risk little to save little. We came to understand that after we left Iraq that the Second Infantry Division's Stryker Combat Team would replace us, and that those would be the last Strykers in Iraq. The people did not want us there. We didn't want to be there. There would be no return on investment for the American soldiers who had sacrificed so much.

# EASTER

IT WAS EASTER SUNDAY at Al Taji. Earlier that day I had opted not to go on a convoy with Alpha Company to deliver mail. Instead, I would spend the holiday evening listening to music and hanging out with my dear friends. Adamowicz and I were binge watching old *Star Trek* episodes on his laptop. It was nice to have someone else who was into geeky things like me. We had been warned that the enemy would choose to strike on Christian holidays. Radicalized Muslims hated Christians. I was unsure that anything would happen but I knew that I didn't want to find out. At 2130 hours on April 12, 2009 Camp Taji came under fire. It happened fast. The EOD teams later determined that we were attacked with a 107 MM Chinese-made rocket fired into our housing area by insurgents. The rocket apparently air burst over the POD area in which I lived.

Just before the attack I was sitting in my room talking to my roommate Adamowicz, being Trekkies. We were talking about home, money, and all the other things that were important to young soldiers like us. It was then that the familiar urge came over me; I had to use the restroom. I walked outside just as I had done a million times before. It was a short jaunt to the latrine—a trailer with four toilets and four shower stalls. I was walking up the latrine stairs when it happened. I heard a light screeching noise and saw what could only be described as a blue streak of light out of the corner of my right eye. A mere fraction of a second later the round impacted the ground with a loud noise and percussion that shook the whole area. It was as if a miniature earthquake had struck us.

Instantly the power went off as the entire housing area went black with darkness. I'm not sure if the rocket knocked out the power or if the base went dark intentionally as a defense mechanism. There was screaming and shouting all around us. Chaos and adrenaline flooded the base as everything seemed to go into slow motion. It was a drunken sluggish feeling. My job then was simple. I had to retrieve my weapon and move to the safety of a concrete bunker. That's exactly what I did.

The medics did an excellent job in making sure that people received any care that they might need. All around us, "Incoming!" was being shouted, screamed, and ordered. Once inside the protective bunker I joined up with my team. That team included Sergeant Adamowicz, Specialist Pearson, Specialist Griffith, and Specialist Mcdonald. There we got right to work. After we obtained good section accountability we assisted the other sections present in and around the bunker with tracking down all of their personnel. Personnel tracking and accountability is an important part of our MOS or job specialty. It is undeniable that my actions contributed to the fast pace in which 100% accountability was reported up our chain of command straight to the brigade level. But most importantly I acted calmly and in accordance with the prescribed rules of engagement under indirect enemy fire. Fortunately no one was hurt from our section in this barrage, though a few purple hearts for injuries would later be issued to other groups on post.

It was over in minutes but as the smoke cleared it felt like much more time had elapsed. Soldiers from Charlie Company of our battalion would have most certainly been injured, if not killed, had they been living in the housing area rather than on mission off post at JSS Hor Al Bash. I thank God each and every day that none of my brothers fell on Easter Sunday. It was truly a day of miracles.

The Chinese-made rockets left shrapnel holes in trailers. Pillows and beds were obliterated. Windows were smashed out of vehicles. The rockets left divots in the ground. But almost as soon as it started, it was all over. The next logical step was to clean up and evaluate all of our material losses. I was no longer just a veteran. I was now a combat veteran, officially. Within a few weeks I was notified that I would receive the Army's Combat Action Badge.

# ONCE A WRESTLER…

**A**NOTHER DAY ON THE Iraqi-side of Camp Taji I was sitting on a couch in a poorly-vented Iraqi Army headquarters building when one of their officers pointed at me and noted that I was a big guy. He asked me if I wanted to wrestle. I didn't have to think long about my decision. The answer was a quick and obvious "no". Whether we were working with the Iraqis or not, I didn't particularly trust them. I knew that wrestling would involve putting down my weapon and placing trust in this foreign national stranger. I didn't want to do it. SGT C. looked at me, obviously pissed off. "Rosado," he said, "don't offend our host, if this man wants to wrestle then wrestle." I couldn't argue with my NCO; he outranked me. SGT C. was an older National Guard soldier, one of the few that had been an E-5 Specialist, before the Army changed its rank structure.

By this time the Arab chitchat was attracting a crowd of Iraqi soldiers who no doubt viewed it as fun way to spend time. I was an oddity in a sort of rag tag militia circus. "Okay" I sighed. I emptied my pockets and handed my sergeant my rifle magazine, which was filled to the brim with thirty rounds of .556-caliber ammunition. I opened my rifle's bipod and set in at the sergeant's feet. I then slowly unzipped my ACU camouflage uniform top and removed it, revealing my wide chest and gut (which was admittedly large by Middle Eastern standards, or even by American standards). They probably thought I was some sort of sheik or royalty in my home country, wealthy enough to be a glutton. I faced the Iraqi officer and leaned forward, placing my hands on my knees, the lifting up my arms so that my hand led in front of me—a defensive amateur-wrestling stance from a good old-fashioned Pennsylvania wrestler.

By this point all of the Iraqi soldiers were laughing at the top of their lungs. Apparently, the Iraq officer's offer wasn't to wrestle, but to arm wrestle. I stood straight up, laughing at the cultural misunderstanding. "No, no no", he laughed as he unbuttoned his uniform top. "We try your way." I knew nothing at all about the capabilities of Iraq in wrestling. I did know that their neighbors in Iran were tough, a major force in international and Olympic competition. But none of that mattered; this was just he and I.

I decided that I would take the offense and shot a low single, driving my shoulder hard into his shin. He fell over but kicked his way out of my grip. I scurried to stand up. This time he advanced towards me, his head hung low, gazing at my boots. I took advantage of his poor posture and snapped down his head hard, cupping his chin in my right hand and pushing my left arm under his with a strong under-hook. I then used the momentum of the match to force him to his back using a move called a cement mixer. He struggled to get free but could not, and then I heard one of the other Americans yell out a deafening, "AT EASE!" I had pinned my opponent, but now standing over me was a tall American sergeant major from the 1st Cavalry Division. He was pissed and demanded my name and unit.

I stood at parade rest, breathing heavily. I answered with my name, rank, and battalion name. "Outside now!" he yelled. I acknowledged him but on the way helped up the Iraqi officer, shaking hands as I went. Outside I was screamed at. The Iraqi soldiers thought it was hilarious, but I was angry. I was told that I had undermined the already frail Iraq Army chain of command and that I might be tried for disrespect of an allied foreign officer. Wrestling didn't scare me; wrestling was part of life since I was a baby. The threat of prison wouldn't scare me if it were Allegheny County prison in Pittsburgh. Those guys had big screen televisions with cable, employment, and free access to education. Fort Leavenworth was much more hardcore. It was a military prison, and the very thought of it scared the hell out of me. Fortunately for me nothing else was ever said about the encounter. I never got into any real trouble beyond a verbal ass chewing.

Every time SGM Stafford asked me to guard prisoners of war I said yes. The Sergeant Major was our most highly-ranked enlisted soldier and a hard man to say no to. It was easy to despise the people that we were guarding. I don't know if they were technically POWs or what the deal was. I knew that they were Iraqi or Syrian, and not much else. Yesterday they were burying roadside bombs or taking pop-shots with their AK-47s at U.S. soldiers. Today they were smoking cigarettes and laughing in a large fenced-in enclosure.

The prisoners didn't seem to have a care in the world. We were feeding them and I think they knew we wouldn't really kill them unless they left us with no other alternative. For them, this was the good life. I kept my finger close to the trigger at all times. A few of the Iraqis tried to make chit chat, asking basic questions. I never answered back. These guys were the enemy and in many respects they were being treated better than we were. A shift guarding prisoners usually lasted between four to six hours. We were on our feet the whole time. It was easy to let your guard down. Without weapons these guys didn't look all that threatening but we all knew that they had been fighting a war against the Western way of living for much longer than our battalion had been at war with them.

One sergeant, Tony Carbone, who seemed to have gone through some sort of substance abuse withdrawal upon his arrival in Iraq, seemed clinically unstable in his treatment of the prisoners. He would often threaten them with a switchblade, or push them around. He reminded me of a Nazi concentration camp commander—not good. I was glad he was on our side though, because he was brutal. I was afraid of him on more than one occasion. A 4TH ID veteran, his unit had found and captured Saddam. He was scary, but good in a fight.

One thing I found remarkable was how willing the prisoners were to give up information to us even though we weren't military intelligence. Who knows if it was reliable—probably not. I suppose some of what was said could have been chalked up to conspiracy theory. They spoke of a great religious revival in the Middle East and upcoming revolutions in neighboring countries like Jordan and Egypt. They predicted a war on both the United States and, somewhat surprisingly, in Israel, that could not be fought with weapons. It was an intriguing lesson in philosophy. It seemed apparent to me that some of these men were not as dumb or uneducated as many took them for. They were mostly proficient in the English language and warned of a future war that would use Christianity's ideals against itself. They threatened to infiltrate us and use our compassion against us. It was a very scary thought. All I knew was that right then, no matter what the future might hold, we had the upper hand. We had the guns. We had the power. For the most part, we had the brains.

I often think about those days of guard duty though, especially when I see a news exposé on rules of engagement. Many of our soldiers that died did so because they were not allowed to fight back like they should have been able to. I'm against war and I'll be the first to admit that, but once you commit to a military conflict you have to give your soldiers the tools that they need not only to survive, but also to thrive and return home alive. Many soldiers and Marines didn't get this benefit. Why shouldn't we decimate our enemies using our technological superiority? War is terrible but if you send an Army to fight for you, let them fight! Our politicians were disconnected. The average U.S. citizen was ignorant. We needed total war—destruction, but that concept was too horrifying to put into practice. The whole world was on fire and the Middle East was the kindling.

# ENEMY AT THE GATES

**M**Y POSITION AS A UNIT mail supervisor gave me access to parts of the post that a lot of guys probably didn't even know were there. I mentioned before that at Camp Taji the base was divided into two huge parts, an Iraq side and an American side. Each side had multiple entry points to gain entrance. U.S. Army members, uniformed contractors, or Ugandans guarded each entrance. I'll never forget one afternoon when I went to the mail warehouse only to find that they weren't ready for me yet. I was early and the incoming shipment had been delayed by weather. I had some time to kill so rather than go back to the tactical operations center I decided instead to explore some of the places on post that I hadn't seen yet. By nature I'm an adventurous guy so seeing new things is all just a part of the fun for me. I was walking near a gate with no helmet or body armor on when I heard an engine accelerating. It sounded like someone really had the pedal to the floor.

A little green hatchback car came zooming toward the gate. The Ugandans started screaming in their native tongue and the next thing I knew I was hearing the snaps, crackles, and pops of gunfire. They opened up on the driver and probably killed the driver but no one friendly died and no unfriendly forces made it onto the post. When I heard the gunshots (which were much louder without ear plugs in) my first reaction was to hit the deck. Realizing that I was unprotected and that this was going on only about 150 meters away, I got onto the ground in the prone position and loaded my thirty-round magazine, chambering a round just in case I had to defend myself. The adrenaline was extreme. Within minutes the military presence at the gate more than tripled as the Quick Response Force arrived along with soldiers who had heard commotion and wanted to see some action.

Fortunately there was no need for me to use my rifle that day. I found out later that the driver had been unarmed, there were no explosives in his vehicle, and all parties involved reacted in a prompt and by-the-book manner. The vehicle *was* his weapon. He charged the gate away from all major traffic flow and he got lit up. Chalk one up for the good guys. The whole event was a harsh reminder for me to reflect on where I was, what I was doing there, and to stay alert.

# MEDIC

**M**OST OF THE GUYS in my battalion had no idea that I had been a volunteer firefighter since I was sixteen years old or that I had extensive vehicle rescue and emergency medical training. I didn't make it a point to tell everyone. I wasn't a medic and if shit hit the fan I wasn't sure that I wanted to be the guy applying tourniquets, so when SSG Chase handed me a combat lifesaver bag due to my Army combat lifesaver certification I took it with hesitation. I didn't want another item to keep track of on my clothing and issue record and I honestly felt like I already had enough on my plate. At the same time, I knew that if I refused it would reflect poorly on my section and on me so I ended up carrying the big bulky bag around. I never once used it.

I only got the chance to use my first responder skills once, while delivering a truckload of mattresses with SGT Tim Smeal on the Iraq side of the post there was a civilian Iraqi woman walking alone on the side of the road. This was a very strange thing to see on the base. In fact it's the only time I saw it. She fell over out of nowhere. I reacted without thinking that it might have been a trap or a ruse. I ran up to her and asked her if she was okay. Her English was weak but she managed to utter a "yeah". She held her ankle. It looked like it was just a twist but I wanted to help her despite there being strict rules about men coming into contact with Iraqi women. The women were viewed more as property than people at that time in that region. There was no such thing as an Iraqi feminist. We were to deal with the oldest male around, as if age and gender equated to rank.

I couldn't help myself though. When I see someone hurting my first inclination is to try to help them. I was assisting her to her feet when two Iraqi soldiers approached me. They were noticeably confused. The woman had my arm in a death grip. An IA guy wearing sergeant rank took my place and she grabbed him. I thanked him and climbed back onto the five-ton Army truck.

As we were driving away I noticed the soldiers push the woman to the ground through the rear view mirror. They had hit her. "Stop the truck," I said. The truck halted. I explained to my driver who outranked me what those assholes had just done; he looked in the mirror to confirm the scene then turned to me. "There's nothing we can do about this but report it, Walt", he said. "Even then, reporting it would probably be worse for the girl than the Iraq Army guys". I had to listen to my sergeant and we drove on, but in many ways I felt I had betrayed my own principles that day. I'm never the guy that runs away from my problems. I'd rather face them head on but that wasn't always possible in Iraq. There were some really awesome Iraq natives that I met and had the chance to interact with on a personal level and then there were some grade A dirt bags.

# MAIL CALL

I TALK ABOUT THE MAIL a lot because in reality it was my primary duty while overseas, but the mail got repetitive fast. I'm not sure most of the soldiers realized what went into it. There was a solid level of risk involved. People from one company might not have understood that I had to handle the correspondence for all of the companies in the battalion, a task that translated to moving thousands of heavy packages. For the most part mail was my show to run as I saw fit, minus a month where SGT Sullivan stepped up until he was made a public relations field photographer. I streamlined the process to a point of near perfection. I had the system so organized that I could do the job myself if I had to but I always preferred the presence of my team. The mail went from being strewn all over a moldy floor under the supervision of the 25TH, to being placed neatly in boxes with a clear system of record keeping.

SGT Sullivan and I were literally among the smartest people in the brigade when it came to mail handling. Jokes and rank aside, I believe that we were the only two people in the entire brigade who were members of MENSA, an organization in which the only requirement was scoring among the top two percent of the world population in a standardized and certified IQ test. We were no joke. Both of us were underutilized. What we accomplished together was a logistics miracle which neither of us ever got credit for. Soon after the deployment, Sullivan left the military and opened a Goin' Postal mailing franchise, similar to a FedEx store, in Tallahassee, Florida, where he has enjoyed great success. I'm very proud to have played such a crucial role in the welfare of battalion morale.

Moving mail meant convoying all the time. Because of IEDs, convoys were the most dangerous part of my life in Iraq. Statistically, for the first time in American military history, drivers had a higher fatality rate than the infantry.

For nine straight months I had been living in a small closet-like trailer known as a combat housing unit or CHU. The time that I spent there was much better than some of the tents that I called home in the three months prior. The best part about my CHU was that it had electricity. This meant I had light to read by and could even write on my laptop occasionally. I didn't have Internet access or much else to do for fun but generally life was good. I still had to go outside and take a short walk to get to a latrine but it could've been much worse. I always thought about how difficult life must have been in World War II. Living in a confined space for so long had a definite psychological effect on me as well as on many of my brothers in arms. I began to feel severe anxiety around any kind of a crowd. In fact, I still have anxiety to some degree today. I'll have feelings of shame and feelings of embarrassment for no real reason. Sometimes I felt completely alone and generally that's how I preferred to be. Fortunately for me the military placed a strong focus on accountability as a constant battlefield practice. I was truly never alone.

Twenty-four hours a day, seven days a week, 365 days a year I was always with someone. Usually it was my sergeant who was also my roommate or one, or both of my fellow specialists. Sometimes I loved the guys and sometimes I hated them. We laughed and we fought. When the order came to clean and retreat from my CHU, I took it as a positive signal that the time to go home was drawing near.

The First Sergeant was a stickler and I had to clean my room several times. I mailed what I wanted to send home back home then I gave most of my personal effects to some of the guys from the unit that would be replacing us and the rest of what I had went into a dumpster to be burned. There was a lot of stuff to get rid of. When I finally did depart from my nest I did so with my body armor and my one bag of belongings, which would have to last me several weeks. At some point in time I learned exactly how to pack and saw the obvious advantage in packing as lightly as possible for troop movements. I handed off my key to the first sergeant who in turn powered down our generators. Then I took one long last walk to surge housing.

My time in Iraq was almost over, and I felt as if I had just gotten there. I had lived through a lot. I had survived mortars, rockets, IEDs, and mounted and dismounted operations. I had flown in military helicopters and in huge cargo planes. I had worked with Rangers, Green Berets, Paratroopers, and SEALs. I wasn't an exceptional soldier. I was just a regular guy. I wasn't the smartest and I wasn't in the best physical shape. I doubted myself often. I learned a lot that I didn't expect to. SPC McDonald taught me how to build furniture from wood (and nice furniture at that!) I played *Guitar Hero* and spray-painted profanities on old Iraqi tanks. I had shady dealings in buying bootleg DVDs, fake Rolex watches, and other things. I tried to make and sell homemade alcohol, a venture that quickly failed due to the odor that emitted from a remote locker space. I did my job, and in a weird way I felt like I would miss Iraq, and certainly the people that I served with.

Everyone was ready to go when it came time to leave Camp Taji. We all reverted to every soldier's true primary occupation—custodian. There was sweeping, mopping, packing, and more that had to be done. 1SGT Deal and Captain Grosinski were solid leaders and even though they were as excited to go home as we were, they were equally dedicated to leaving our living area in better condition than it was left to us. This is something that the 28TH Division always takes it upon themselves to do that many other divisions do not. Cleaning is a part of life that seems rarely mentioned in books about war, but in reality cleaning occupied a lot of our time. You can't do too much cleaning. I've found that many junior non-commissioned officers would have their guys clean when there was nothing else to do because it made them look proactive and kept the soldiers busy. Many times this was unnecessary but, like I said, it's all just part of life as an enlistee in the armed forces.

Many of our Stryker crews left the post early in order to convoy the heavy troop carrier Stryker vehicles back into Kuwait where they would board huge naval ships. I was not among these soldiers. Not having the Strykers there for us to use in Iraq made many of us feel naked. They were our whole reason for being and the point of the sword for all of our infantry missions in country. The Stryker had been heavily criticized but it worked well for us and in our case, it definitely saved lives.

Those of us who remained out of Headquarters Company filed into temporary barracks and prepared for an aerial movement to Baghdad. The year had gone by quickly. We would soon make every movement that we made to get to Taji, Iraq again, but in reverse.

# SURGE HOUSING

**S**URGE HOUSING WAS A temporary barracks area meant to hold a large number of incoming soldiers until more permanent billets could be acquired. It was never meant to work in reverse. Nevertheless, that was where we were heading. Surge housing was a humongous warehouse-style structure with what looked like thin panels of aluminum siding for walls. It was as hot as hell inside and we all slept on bunk beds with less than one foot of distance in between each bed set. The housing was built for efficiency, not comfort. Outside there was a huge line of portable toilets and a trailer of sinks for us to shave and wash up before going to sleep. The trailer ran out of water only hours after being filled. There were the familiar concrete mortar shelters outside, however I was doubtful that all 800+ of us would have fit into these mortar barriers should we have taken fire as we had earlier in the year on Easter.

I hoped to use the week living in surge to sleep, relax, and reload. By that point my office had been torn down and all of my responsibilities had been successfully handed off to the First Battalion 82nd Field Artillery of the First Cavalry Division, the unit that had replaced my own battalion. For the first time in a year, I had nothing to do. Rather than get an opportunity to rest I was instead pulled from surge housing and put onto various work details, which lasted all day, and every day. Most of the stuff I had to do probably should've fallen under the jurisdiction of the supply and logistics soldiers. Supply and human resources typically ran side by side in the enlisted world, or at least that's what my experience dictated. I was sent to help them track down and turn in all sorts of equipment and hardware. One of the supply section zone enlisted soldiers and other backfills from a far off unit boycotted work for those final days. They felt that they were being used inappropriately and may have had a point. Their actions meant another grouping of soldiers like me had to step up and make up the ground lost by service members with similar mentalities. They had mentally checked out. Doing these menial tasks did not bother me in the slightest. What did bother me was the fact that we were so often asked to clean up after another battalion, the 'Associators', the First, and 111TH infantry battalion out Philadelphia, Pennsylvania. I had to pick up garbage around dumpsters that were located nowhere near where I had lived. It was a very dirty job.

Walking back from a detail one day, I stopped off at a MWR recreational facility to take a break. There were seven of my fellow soldiers from one of the personal security detachments hiding out to avoid being detected for these details. All of their NCO leaders were there protecting their guys from having to do extra work. Secretly I wished that some of my leaders looked after me like that. Of course seeing them all resting there led me to follow suit. I sat down and rested for a good twenty minutes, nearly gave into exhaustion and fell asleep, and then faced the music and returned to the surge housing area.

It was an extremely stressful environment but you did what you had to in hopes that all of the additional efforts would make things move more smoothly later. I ate food whenever I could but that amounted to less than once every two days. When I did finally get the chance to dine I wasn't exactly eating healthy. I was eating for taste and comfort. The thought that kept me going was the idea that everything I was doing was to go home and that the sooner it was done, the faster I would find myself back home, happy, and on American soil.

# THE FLIGHT LINE

**A**LL OF MY EFFORTS AT surge housing paid off. Soon enough, I was on the back of the two and a half ton truck heading to the empty field that would serve as a makeshift landing zone for massive Chinook helicopters. I managed to fit everything I owned into a single duffel bag with the intention of making the voyage as simple on myself as was humanly possible. As an unexpected "reward" for my foresight, I had to carry two bags belonging to a young officer who must have had a packing strategy completely opposite to my own.

We were not allowed to wear hats on the flight line. We all sat on the hot, dusty ground in a huge cluster talking and waiting for hours a time. There was an awful lingering odor that smelled something like ass and cat urine. Given the limited hygiene opportunities afforded to us I suppose that the odor was to be expected. Those days were some of the hottest in the region that we had seen to date and everyone was sweating profusely while waiting for the order to move.

When darkness fell, moments passed before we heard the familiar buzz and chop of helicopter blades beating against the hard, warm air. At first nothing was visible in the sky. Then, as if out of nowhere, the Chinooks appeared. They were huge, glorious birds of liberty that would free us from the chains of Army life in Iraq as well as from the oppression of the infantry regiment. We boarded the aircraft in chalks of twenty men per trip, plus gear. We ran up the helicopter ramp against the heat and wind and squeezed into the chopper as tightly as possible. We accomplished these loading tasks with unprecedented speed and precision—you could tell that we were motivated to go home.

We were literally sitting on each other's laps and laughing about it the whole time. We were in the air for only fifteen minutes or so. The flight was short but turbulent, and to me it felt like we were hovering especially low. It ended swiftly when we touched down at Baghdad International Airport. The last time I that I had been in Baghdad had been over nine months ago.

# BAGHDAD
# INTERNATIONAL
# AIRPORT

L EAVING IRAQ WAS VIRTUALLY the exact process that we
went through when entering the country, but in reverse. We were
first taken to what was called the Stryker stables. Stryker stables
were tents that sat isolated on the outskirts of Camp Liberty in the
province of Baghdad, Iraq. Here finally I could rest.

I slept in, went to the gym and the PX, and used the time to browse
through merchandise that the Baghdad vendors were permitted to
sell on post. I only had to check in with my NCOs once a night, typically at 8:00 PM. There were no details or small jobs for us to do in
Bagdad. Here we were finally the guests. We had restrooms and shower
trailers available for use. Luxury did not necessarily make life safer,
though. The showers were made of steel and several soldiers from
other units had died from electrical shocks in similar trailers since
the war began in 2003. I consider those shower fatalities both pre-

ventable and unnecessary. At least one of these deaths was a Pennsylvania man from Allegheny County, near my hometown.

Colonel Flanagan made sure that each company made it very clear to the soldiers that we were not out of the woods yet. We were still Iraq. We were still in danger. We were not to speak about where we were, where we had been, the things we had done, or where we were from. Any of these seemingly meaningless bits of information could result in harm to us, our comrades, or even our families. Basic information was time and again intercepted for use against us by an intelligent enemy presence. It was the "loose lips sink ships" mentality that helped keep us safe. Some people broke these rules. Maybe it made a difference, maybe not.

My favorite part of Baghdad International Airport this time around was that I could go to the Post Exchange area and buy "graninis", a fruit drink filled with vitamins and flavor served in a large pineapple-shaped container. Little treats like this made life in Iraq taste all the sweeter and more bearable.

No one could receive mail anymore now that we were on the move, but mail still played an important part in our lives in that we could mail letters home telling our loved ones to get ready. Soon we'd be with them. We weren't to give specifics or say exactly when we were coming but we were coming nonetheless. Eventually the newspapers back home would let the secret out. The Pennsylvania boys had done their time.

After several days the call came. We amassed in yet another field, this time the aircraft of choice being the mighty C130. This is the same humongous plane that men parachute from at the U.S. Army's Airborne School. We were packed in tightly amongst both gear and pallets of equipment. In keeping with protocol we only moved during the nighttime. It was safer. In the air I slept, exhausted by the stress of it all. The flights were short yet worthwhile and before the sun rose we were no longer in Iraq. We were now back in Kuwait. What a differ-ence a border makes!

Anyone who observed us during troop movements was in awe of our speed, competency, and professionalism. We had learned to work together well over the past months. We were a family, albeit a some-what dysfunctional one. But it was time to go home.

# ALI AL SALEM

**A**LI AL SALEM WAS an Australian post in Kuwait. The base could easily be swallowed up by the surrounding desert if it weren't for the human efforts to push back against Mother Nature each and every day. An Australian base meant Australian women—a hot commodity for the lonely American infantrymen of the 112TH who had endured a rough year. Many guys tried to pick up an Australian female soldier or two. Most failed but you've got to strike out every once in awhile if you want to hit home runs. We wouldn't be in Ali Al Salem for long.

Baghdad was an allied stronghold and the capital of Iraq. The soldiers that served there felt fairly secure. Few, if any of them, walked around wearing body armor. I might dare to go as far as saying that they were a bit complacent. Whenever there was an explosion in the town (bombings seemed to be the most impactful enemy weapon in that area) the U.S. seemed slow to react. This inadequacy was explained away as an after effect of the forced transition of power from the U.S. Army back to the Iraqi Army. The U.S. Army would not intervene without being specifically requested by the local government.

I strongly disagreed with this mantra because in my eyes any action that destabilized the region also endangered allied troops that were serving there. It was obvious that the infantry battalions were disappearing. We would be one of the last. Media attention was shifting almost entirely to Afghanistan even though there were still Americans being killed in action in Iraq. It might show our ignorance for our political leaders to believe that they could fix a problem that transcends our own military scope in Middle Eastern history.

The area in which we stayed in Kuwait was immaculately clean, a fact which we found both surprising and refreshing. The Kuwaiti standard of living was very high. This was because all of the citizen-residents were entitled to a share of the profits from the gross national product. That product for Kuwait was oil. The smallest house that I saw in Kuwait would've been among the largest mansions in a wealthy Pittsburgh neighborhood. We left one by one as we boarded large coach tour buses with blacked out windows and curtains to reduce visibility. The people of Kuwait liked to keep the foreign militaries out of sight and out of mind. On the bus we were treated to bottles of gourmet water—in a bottle and free of sediment—a welcome change. The voyage to the next base would last a little under an hour's time. We traveled using what were essentially super highways. About every 2 miles on this road, however, there was a pickup soccer game going on, literally in the middle of the road. Large groups of people were playing smack dab in the middle of the roadways.

The sun was high in the sky by the time we reached the post. There we received yet another speedy in-brief and were shown to our tents, where we would be residing for the next several days. The best part of Kuwait was that they had a McDonald's. There, the going price for a cheeseburger was just under $7.00 American—a ridiculous sum of money for a burger at that time. Still, many of the guys in my company were glad to pay any price for taste of home. I'm sure that the Kuwaitis knew this. I was getting tired of portable toilets and MRE meals myself.

It was in Kuwait that I got closer to a few different soldiers. There I had three roommates: Captain Ogden, a graduate of my President's Athletic Conference rival school Washington and Jefferson College and an Afghanistan vet and a signal officer; Specialist Sturgill who was called out of the inactive reserve after a one-year hiatus to serve his country one more time; and Specialist Talasky, one of the craziest yet good-hearted men I've ever met my lifetime. The four of us were left to live in a huge tent by ourselves after Alpha Company of the First Battalion 112TH Infantry pushed ahead to Germany before us. We chatted and shared stories, laughed, and perhaps most importantly made our final packing preparations. I loved having a limited number of personnel near the end because it meant less work details and less noise. It was generally quiet. There was none of the outgoing artillery fire or gunfire that we had all grown so accustomed to.

The next step was to a board yet another aircraft, but first we had to go through an extensive customs process. In Kuwait, the United States Navy ran and operated the military customs detachment. They were very thorough, though it turned what could've taken twenty minutes with an x-ray machine into an eight-hour venture. When I threw my last duffel bag onto the long dark conveyor belt I felt a huge weight lift off of my shoulders both figuratively and literally. I would not have to handle my bag again until I was back in the United States.

We sat in a large tent until it was time to board the plane. Our aircraft this time was a huge civilian Boeing 747. We filled every seat. I sat next to young sergeant from Charlie Company. International flights were always the same. Military flights are no different than civilian flights except you had a rifle on your lap. I mostly slept until the plane touched down in Germany.

Germany looked exactly like Pennsylvania. There were trees, foliage, grass, and women. Most noticeable was the green vegetation all around. It was to be sure a sight for sore eyes. We weren't in the desert anymore.

We spent an hour at the terminal. I didn't know exactly where in the country that I was but I knew that it was a much different airport than the one that we had stopped in nearly a year earlier when making our initial push into Iraq via Kuwait. I know this because I had hoped to purchase some absinthe from the European vendor that I had seen earlier in the tour. I was disappointed that I would miss the opportunity, however we were in a much different place. There was no booze. Our plane was hot and stunk much as you would imagine 220 men would smell like having not showered in a week. The aircraft had recently gone through an extensive refueling process that left a light gasoline-like odor in the air as well. Because we were about to depart for long flight across the Atlantic Ocean, our civilian flight crew didn't want to take any unnecessary risk. We wouldn't move until the smell had been investigated and eliminated, the synthetic smell at least.

This made a lot of guys overly anxious, including myself, but when it came down to it I would rather have spent another week in Germany than to have had my plane go down in the middle of the Atlantic Ocean. We sat in the airplane waiting for takeoff for nearly six whole hours. A shot of Jack Daniels would have been nice. Most guys got more irritable by the second. What we all wanted was to get off of the plane and stretch our legs but that didn't happen. The flight crew did their best to make things easier on us but it didn't help. They withheld information about when we might depart and cracked terrible jokes in what seemed to be a last ditch effort to keep us from killing each other or perhaps even our flight attendant crew. I know that even then I started to display some of the angry emotions that would mildly affect me when I returned home. One of the flight attendants offered a plausible explanation for all the confusion when she mentioned that our pilot was "ex-Navy".

We sat there frustrated for what felt like forever. The flight home had a significantly different feel than the flight to Iraq, largely because so many of us who were psychologically fine when we departed for Iraq now had severe PTSD. On the upside, the airline had opted to show new movies on the in-flight televisions that we had not had the privilege of knowing were even out. Most of the movies hadn't been yet released for DVD production in the United States but a special airline contract allowed them to show these videos to us. They were of much better quality than the bootlegs that we purchased at Istaqlal or Al Taji Market. We finally lifted off in what would otherwise be an uneventful flight to New Jersey.

# ARRIVAL AT MCGUIRE AIR FORCE BASE

**T**HE PLANE LET OUT A FAINT metallic hum as the landing gear began to lower. Everyone was excited when the pilot had announced that we were above Canada. Now we were all eagerly looking out of the small porthole-shaped windows. What was below us transitioned quickly from Canada to the United States. Our plane had begun its final approach. The uncomfortable, cramped flight seemed to last forever. The pilot and lead flight attendant had cracked terrible jokes throughout the duration of the voyage and, despite having perhaps the best intentions, left many bitter. Now they were making up for it in a huge way. They were taking us home.

When the wheels finally connected with the ground, offering a slight burst of turbulence, all of the guys were clapping, cheering, or letting out some type of smart-ass remark. Our medics could always be counted on for jackass comments. On the ground we waited patiently for twenty minutes to disembark. When the hatch finally opened, all of us were ready to roll out with gear in hand. We had one final descent to make: down a narrow stairwell. When my boot touched American soil I felt overjoyed. If there wasn't a long line of soldiers both in front of and behind me I would have dropped to my knees and kissed the ground in the fashion of Pope John Paul II.

We had to shake hands with a line of people, which included the Adjutant General of the Pennsylvania National Guard and the general in charge of the division. We also got to see our advanced party who had left Iraq weeks before us to prepare Fort Dix for our arrival. I was so glad to see Sergeants Fassette and Adamowicz. I'd missed them both. I was most honored to shake the hand of a young member of the engineer corps. When we were in Iraq he had narrowly survived an IED attack, losing his right arm and left leg, along with other body damage. Most of the guys didn't think he would make it, and there he was. He was already walking on prosthetics and his girlfriend was right by his side. I felt terrible for the guy, but out of all the high-ranking people in that welcome line he was the one I was most humbled and honored to see. It could have been anybody. Here he was surviving, and with grace. He was a beacon of pride to us all. The weather in New Jersey caught me off guard. It wasn't near the 130 plus degrees that it was in Iraq but I was still sweating like crazy. It wasn't the dry heat of Central Iraq, either. I was finally reintroduced to humidity.

We were bused to a huge garage where we were encouraged to turn in our M4 assault rifles. Not having a rifle by my side made me feel naked. Every place I stopped I would check to see if I had my weapon, only to remind myself that all was well—it was back in the government's hands. Shortly after going home I would buy a Bushmaster AR-15 because I felt so much more comfortable with an assault rifle by my side than without. I wasn't especially pro-gun, but I now felt unsteady without a firearm. Today I look at the Second Amendment as one of the constitutional rights most in need of and worthy of defending. There was a Fort Dix/McGuire Air Force Base in-processing briefing and a short ceremony for men whose families made the drive from Pennsylvania and from all around the country. I wish someone had told me that I could invite my family! There wasn't anyone there to welcome me home.

Of course the backfill stigma ran true, even though I was largely now accepted a a part of the unit. We were then shuttled to our barracks where all were appreciative of the steady water pressure and flushing toilets. The demobilization process was about to begin.

# DEMOBILIZATION

**F**OR THE FIRST TIME in a long while there was downtime. Demobilization is basically a big box that the Army has to check when reserve component soldiers return home. It comes at you in shifts. The first wave is called CIF and is where we turned in essential equipment that the government required for the war effort. The only big-ticket expensive item that we had to part with was our body armor. There were about seven different acronyms for body armor and I didn't know, or care, what many of the acronyms stood for. The Army loves to use acronyms, even if they confuse things. The IOTV replaced the IBA as the premier body armor of NATO forces at the time. It was pulled down over our heads like a hooded sweatshirt rather than one arm at a time, like a windbreaker (the old style), and included small plates, which protect your sides when shooting. It also had a quick release so that soldiers could get free of it if their vehicle would roll over in water, a safeguard to avoid drowning. It was nearly two pounds lighter than the last version and was a major battlefield innovation. No one in the world had anything better for personal protection. Even though our mission was ending, our vest would return immediately to the deserts of Iraq and the hills of Afghanistan for instant service. That part of us would fight on.

We had to go through vast medical and dental screening and make sure our financial affairs were in order. Men that had drank Rip It, a sugary citrus energy drink that was made readily available to us in Iraq, typically had trouble passing the dental evaluation. There were no psychological evaluations; a point, which I felt, was a big miss on the part of the Army.

The best part of demobilization was a forty-five minute gripe session with a high-ranking chaplain. Popular topics included living conditions, leadership, and stress. A seasoned medic named Chaterjji nearly made the chaplain cry with his brutal honesty about things that were done unsafely.

At nighttime we were all excited to use the New Jersey phones and internet. We ordered pizza and Chinese food and tried to indulge in some of the small luxuries that we had gone without for so long. When we finalized the process by validating our Department of Defense Form 214, a formal release from active duty, we were back in the National Guard. I was always surprised that the Army never made me, or offered to me the chance to speak with a psychologist about everything that we had gone through. I'm sure that my words cannot possibly do justice to the stress and emotions that occurred during our time in Iraq.

# GOODBYE 112TH

I WAS CURIOUS TO SEE how saying goodbye to my comrades would play out. There were a few people that I knew I would miss almost immediately but there were also certainly people that I hoped I would never again cross paths with. There were mixed feelings, to say the least.

Would there be hugging, crying, or handshakes? The backfill soldiers, like me, were mustered out of service from the battalion following a series of small formalities. No one really spoke about the fact that we wouldn't be seeing each other anymore until just before that final moment of departure. It was quiet with random spatters of humor and comedy, the elements that helped us grunts relieve stress throughout the tour. When the time finally came, the goodbye charge was led by my NCO in charge, Sergeant First Class Anderson who hugged me, said "I'll miss you bitch", and promised that I'd be getting orders in the mail soon to transfer to their unit. It was a rough joke given the circumstances. I hugged a couple of the guys in my section but was disappointed that I missed out on saying goodbye to Captain Smith, who was undergoing urgent gallbladder surgery, and Sergeant Sullivan, the IRR soldier from Florida who had already moved forward—both great guys.

Sergeant Adamowicz insisted that I give him a phone call when I got my cellular phone turned back on. Staff Sergeant Fassette flexed, saying something crazy about getting a WWE professional wrestling contract. We were all the same stupid kids that we were the previous September when all of this was just starting out, just a little bit better adapted to thriving in the presence of ignorance. We were a family in the truest sense. We weren't like the Brady Bunch—we were real.

And then it was over. I rejoined with others heading to Pittsburgh. These guys were family too. That's when I realized something very important about the armed forces: no matter where you are on the globe you have a family in your brothers and sisters in uniform.

# HIGHWAY TO HEAVEN

THERE WERE ONLY FIVE of us standing outside the Fort Dix barracks. Only five soldiers were Pittsburgh-bound out of a brigade of several thousand. It wasn't a surprise when the organic soldiers (the men that belonged to the regiment from the get-go and weren't assigned from somewhere else as I was) loaded onto their buses and headed for home. We stood there and watched as they left. It made sense that they would be released first. Over the past few months I had become a firm believer in Murphy's Law, the credo that declares that anything that can go wrong will go wrong.

It took a while but our fifteen-passenger government van eventually showed up. With at least two duffel bags per man we had more baggage aboard the van than personnel. I sat in between Nick Lehota and Kevin Rock, an infantryman and a mechanic, and two good friends. Also in the van were SFC George DeEsch, SGT Sean Mike Cavanaugh, and Captain Paul Ogden. Some of us were sporting our new 82nd Airborne Division combat patches. Only our Alpha Company and Headquarters Company had earned the right to wear it out of the entire brigade, but the brigade's leaders tried to suppress its wear out of jealousy, or some other petty feeling. Now outside of the scope of the 56TH Brigade we were free to wear it.

For the first half hour or so we tried to talk amongst ourselves. We quickly found that after a year together there wasn't a whole lot we had left to talk about. On the road we were all excited to see the Bat Boat from the 1960's Batman television series on a trailer. You know you're in America when one of Batman's vehicles is next to you on the highway.

The trip from New Jersey to Pittsburgh took a few hours and our driver broke it up with three stops at rest areas. I took the chance to indulge in a latte from Starbucks and to speak to some appreciative civilians, including a little boy who declared that someday he wanted to be "just like me". I even posed for a few pictures with people. When the Ohio River came into sight my heart rate jumped. This was Pittsburgh. I was home.

Even today I can't say it enough; I was home!

# STANDING DOWN AT THE 128TH

**M**ANY SOLDIERS FROM MY home unit were waiting at the 128TH FSB in Pittsburgh when I arrived. I was home and felt immediately welcomed by my organic unit. Some of them were envious of the combat patch but most were just friendly. I wondered if later they would value my service as a trigger-puller, or if I'd be barred from promotion in the Good Ol' Boys Club of those who had bonded in staying behind. They had so few people that knew how to react in the fog of war. It was a far cry from the infantry regiment.

My grandmother showed up to pick me up with her friend Annette. Gram was in tears. Her boy was home. She told me that every time she would hear or read the word/name "Walter" in a book or movie that she knew I was thinking of her. My mom's cancer was now terminal; she was unable to make the trip. Other units had big gala events with fire departments, motorcycles, and media. All we had was a few family members. But I wouldn't have had it any other way. The unit hadn't changed at all. Everything was the same but at the same time everything looked better. I couldn't get over it. I was home!

# FROM FOXHOLES TO FREE LUNCHES

**D**URING ONE OF COLONEL Flanagan's glorious motivational speeches he told us all to wear our uniforms when we got home. He said that he often eats for free when he's at home and that many people are more than willing to treat service members to special perks and gratuities. Upon first hearing him say this, most of the men uttered things like "must be nice" under their breath. High-ranking officers make much more money than the average private. I didn't want to be a leech when I got home. I was tired of wearing a uniform. I just wanted to grow a nice beard and relax, maybe even smoke a blunt. Not many people were quick to accept thanks for what they did. Even the guys who never fired a shot had spent an entire year away from their family and loved ones. We were all thrown into a terrible place with some pretty dangerous people (on both sides). Few, if any, returned home satisfied with their deployment experiences with the 56TH Brigade.

Instead of being eager to self-congratulate most soldiers said things like, "We didn't do that much" or "Our awards are a joke." I think this is very sad. Most of it comes from older soldiers who exaggerated their prior deployments. Those soldiers received combat awards so they elevate the tension in their stories to paint themselves as heroes. The younger soldiers latched onto the words of their respected NCO leaders and a huge negative smear campaign of all "end of tour" awards ensued. It left younger soldiers feeling useless. It's a truly tragic, repeating occurrence. A full bird Colonel, Marc Ferraro, who was likely next in line in the division to be promoted to Brigadier General, interpreted the U.S. Army official awards regulation to make an educated determination on all combat awards. I guess he felt it was all deserved. Full Bird Colonel is a term used to describe Colonels in the Army, whereas Lieutenant Colonels are often called "Light Colonels". I would return very highly decorated, at least for a soldier of my rank and experience level.

Within an hour of being home, Grandma wanted to take me out to lunch, not to honor me but just to feed me. I was hungry! At Atria's Restaurant in Fox Chapel, a wealthy suburb, I ate bread and veal and crab. I drank fresh milk and juice. We both basically stuffed our faces. As we got ready to leave three of the waitresses came over, saying things like, "Thank you for your service" and eventually, "This meal's on us". It was an incredible gesture on their part and made me feel pretty good.

I don't feel guilty when someone says thank you anymore. Now I just say "You're welcome". I would find out later that the woman at the restaurant's son, Tony Karpinski, had gone to my high school and was now a member of my home battalion. It's a small world.

# G20: THE BATTLE
# FOR THE BURG

**A** GREAT MANY PEOPLE around the country rank Pittsburgh among the top cities to live in. It's true that the once industrial powerhouse has a lot going on. There are sports, stage shows, gambling, museums, restaurants, nightclubs, and much more in the Steel City. Even so, Pittsburgh is smashed into a narrow valley. It feels like almost every street is one way and it's hard for even residents to get around on occasion. Names like Carnegie, Mellon, and Warhol brought the city fame but in my opinion, Pittsburgh can't quite stack up to New York, Boston, or Chicago when it comes to the number of things that you can do.

Only a few short days after my return, Pittsburgh caught the nation's eye by welcoming the world for the G20 summit. The G20 is an international forum of leaders from emerging and industrialized economies, coming together to discuss issues and try to fix what they can. Overall I don't think the G20 summit accomplished very much. Pittsburgh probably wasn't big enough to host an event that required such stringent security due to President Obama and other world leaders attending. Security was at the highest level I had ever seen in Allegheny County.

Here's how it crippled the city:

- Most major businesses operating out of the downtown area closed, missing out on days of potential profits.

- The river system consisting of the Allegheny, Ohio, and Monongahela rivers was shut down to all non-commercial traffic.

- Roads and city grids were re-tasked, making it hard for both citizens to get around and for essential services like fire departments and ambulances from reaching their destinations with optimal speed.

Things that I never expected to see happen in Pittsburgh did. While driving across a bridge I was stunned to see a group of masked protesters jump over its side using ropes and harnesses to suspend both themselves and giant banners just feet above the water. They looked like ninjas dressed in dark colors and hanging from the long strings. They weren't protesting the war, the summit, religious issues, or civil rights. They just wanted to save the environment.

A string of vandalism ensued in the more urban areas. Youthful protesters smashed out windows of business and disrupted everyday life. Police agencies from all over Pennsylvania and several other states showed up in force and the National Guard was mobilized. A short string of Hummers slid past the baseball stadium. I couldn't help think of Iraq. It didn't look so different. Many of the protesters were young college-age students. I was personally activated to service, armed and placed under the command of a Chicago police officer that was in Pittsburgh for the event. It was martial law.

One night at the University of Pittsburgh, a huge group of students took to the streets. Some protesters were causing problems and the students were eager to be part of the whole historic event. When the riot squads arrived on scene, all of the kids that had amassed were chanting, "We love Pittsburgh, fuck G20!" The police assembled in a phalanx formation to sweep the students up the street and opened fire with tear gas canisters and beanbag non-lethal rounds fired from 12 gauge shotguns. Some of the targets were young girls, probably averaging 17 and 18 years of age who were likely just caught up in the spectacle of the summit.

On another front, in the Lawrenceville district of Pittsburgh, armored vehicles prowled the streets using new non-lethal weapons—ultrahigh noise frequencies to disrupt crowds. Electronic translators issued out orders in English, Polish, and Spanish through a deep robotic voice. As a platoon of soldiers marched down the street, some of the people of Pittsburgh were sitting in front of their houses in lawn chairs cheering them on. Hearing things like "Kick those hippies' asses, boys!" as the warriors passed was fairly typical. If you went for a jog or to the store and didn't have two forms of identification you could be detained. It felt very much like a combat zone. It was a police state for the duration of the summit.

What the hell was this? Was it reality? Is this what we fought over there for? It was discouraging and confusing. The military occupation of Iraq proved that the U.S. Armed Forces could be deployed in a long-term occupation and police action. Pittsburgh G20 showed that the government was not above using this military prowess at home, regardless of the constitutional implications.

# SLEEPLESS NIGHTS

**S**LEEPING IS A FUNNY THING. Sometimes there's nothing better than a good night's sleep. Dreams can even make sleep enjoyable. While I was in Iraq, I never dreamt. This could have been because of the external noise we were subjected to, or the strange hours, or the stress—I don't know.

Throughout my life I've had a few recurring nightmares that have caused me grief. I think everyone has them. In one, I'm in my junior high school. Class is about to start and I'm by the lockers in a busy hallway. I don't know which locker is mine. I think I know the general area but I'm coming up short time and again. To make things worse all of the lockers have combination locks on them. I can't find my locker so I panic.

In another dream I'm entirely conscious but unable to move while lying down. I use every ounce of mental power to move a finger, even a little bit, but I cannot move.

In another my teeth crumble in my head and I struggle to spit them out.

Since I returned home the frequency of these dreams increased. I don't know why. I also have other dreams. Dreams where events in Iraq had different consequences than they did in real life. It's horrific. I think a part of those dreams are guilt that I felt. When I'm reading the *Army Times* and I see that more young soldiers have fallen overseas I tend to focus on what makes me different from them. I wasn't any better. I was just more fortunate. There is a level of mental strain involved with leaving home and dealing with stress. My dreams reminded me of where I had been and motivated me to improve. They are a part of me now. Sleeping an entire night is an extremely rare thing for me and others like me. For a veteran, the war does not end.

# SECURING THE FUTURE

**W**ITH ELEVEN MONTHS of deployment dwell time before I could be activated again, and being on leave until December, I decided to get right back in the saddle with my life. I started exercising more regularly, ordering the P90X workout videos and purchasing a gym membership and supplements. I wanted to look and feel much better than I did.

My next concern was my financial security. I invested only six of the thirty-six thousand dollars I made during my year in Iraq into my stock portfolio. I wanted to put much more in but the market and overall economy were doing poorly and were unpredictable to say the least. I played it safe and put the investment into a prominent mutual fund. I didn't feel comfortable with the trillions of dollars in national debt that had amassed.

Over the past two years I had lost nearly ten thousand dollars due to the market. Consumer confidence extremely low due to the political decisions that were being made in the U.S., especially those that were being made regarding interest rates by the U.S. Federal Reserve. I was a long-term investor so I'm very accepting of loss and gain due to trends. I was ever confident that things would get better. I didn't buy any savings bonds because I figured I was too young for that type of investment and the value of the American dollar was wavering. I started a coin collection as both a good investment and a hobby. I mostly collected gold and silver pieces, as bullion holds its own in hard times. Gold had never been valued at zero and had nearly tripled in value the previous few years. Once I felt that my health and financial futures were secure, I turned to academics.

Unfortunately because of the awkward time I returned home I had to miss almost an entire semester of school. I wouldn't be able to return to my graduate studies until January, a long wait. When I did finally make it back I had more federal education funding than ever. I could go to school for very little in terms of out of pocket expense, but everything else in life seemed to cost a lot of money. I had to wear regular cloths, not government provided uniforms. I had to again pay rent and buy food. My wages were again taxed—I wasn't overseas anymore—and an onslaught of bills ensued. Uncle Sam squeezed every cent he could from me. I had to watch my finances very closely but it was otherwise business as usual. It was hard being home. It was stressful and it was hard. I really missed the active duty military and often yearned for that lifestyle and for the fraternity that was offered by my teammates. I would often look at the wads of paper that eventually became the basis for this book. In reading I would laugh, cry, and remember. I had done something amazing and important that year. I represented my country and my values as a deployed soldier in a war against the evil of global terrorism. Now I was home, and trying to learn how to be ordinary again.

# PROVING GROUNDS

I GUESS I COULDN'T STAY away from military bases for too long. My brother had a 4-day pass from his Advanced Individual Training and we hadn't seen each other in over a year so I decided to make the five-hour drive to see him at Aberdeen Proving Grounds in Maryland. Rusty had followed in my footsteps and enlisted into the Army. He was the distinguished honor graduate from his class at the Army's Ordnance Corps School. He looked like a different person than when I last saw him. He was skinny as a rail and I was proud of him for making such positive changes in attitude.

"What do you want to do while I'm here?" I asked him. "It's up to you," he sighed. I chose Gettysburg. Only an hour and minutes away from the Maryland post there are many lessons to be learned from the Civil War battlefield. We went on the tours, shopped in the stores, and touched monuments on the field. The Army War College sends top-tier leaders there to study strategy, as does West Point, VMI, The Citadel, and Annapolis. There's so much to learn from the fields that one could spend a lifetime observing them. I get teary eyed every time

I think about the events that transpired there and the many men who gave their lives for a slew of causes in 1863.

I wanted to reinforce to my brother that our job was not a game. It was serious business. We are sometimes asked to commit terrible acts. Many pay the ultimate price for the American way of life. It was great to see my brother again. He was making all kinds of plans for relationships, work, school, a house. I encouraged him to just take things one day at a time. He told me I should take some of my own advice and do the same. He showed maturity I hadn't seen from him in a long time.

We scaled Little Round Top overlooking Devil's Den and imagined what it could have been like, we threw back beers at the Dobbin House Tavern, and we ran the trails near the college there. The weekend ended almost as soon as it started and he returned to Aberdeen Proving Grounds to spend some time in the field and prepare for graduation. He was on his own journey; different from mine yet somehow intertwined. I secretly worried about his future. Had I done my job well enough to keep him out of Iraq? Hell, would our children and grandchildren fight in Iraq? It was beyond my control. I had proven myself. I suspected that he would too, either in war, or life. It was in this moment that I saw the cyclic nature of war and the military. I realized that there was nothing that I could do to prevent the next generation from going to war, but maybe the next generation could learn something from my story that might help them to cope with what they might have to endure, either as combat arms or support soldiers. I was all too happy, and proud, to share my story.

# SHARING THE LESSONS: FAQ

W HEN I WAS AN UNDERGRAD in college I was a history major. I did okay at first but I did much better when I learned how to study as a team. Between education classes, history classes, and other liberal arts requirements, I needed my friends. They weren't just a social luxury, but also an academic resource. During my freshman year I studied with a small group consisting of Kayla, Allison, Pat, Jeff, and Tim. All of them remain my friends today. Tim Mengle went on to be a high school teacher at Norwin High School in Western Pennsylvania. One weekend he called me. He was doing a class on combat through the ages and wanted to know if I would do a teleconference with the class and answer any questions they might have over Skype. I was happy to oblige. Here are a few of the questions that I was asked and the answers I came up with at the time.

## DO YOU AGREE WITH THE U.S. INVASION OF IRAQ?

Yes I do, if for no other reason than because Saddam Hussein was committing genocide against his own people. Evils such as genocide should never be tolerated by a country that is driven by principles of freedom and with the power to do something about it, like the United States. As Americans, we have a moral obligation to act. One problem I have with the argument of justice as it relates to the United States is that we pick and choose which dictators to act against and which ones to ally with without standardization. I believe that the occupation of both Iraq and Afghanistan will be strategically important in a future where Iran is poised for dominance over the Middle East and in striking distance of a nuclear capability. I was not involved in the initial 2003 Iraq invasion. I was in high school like you. I think future generations will scrutinize our reasons for deploying, however you can't change the past. You can learn from mistakes and work towards a brighter future, however.

## WHAT DO YOU THINK ABOUT WOMEN IN THE MILITARY?

I think that women are an integral part of the Armed Forces. I would suggest that anyone that disagrees meet soldiers like Lesley Schneider, a radio communications specialist that was attached to the 112TH and could run circles around most of the male soldiers. The Army does their best to separate female soldiers from the bulk of combat operations by excluding them from certain jobs, such as the infantry. There are no female infantrymen. There are no women Rangers. This will change soon, and rightfully so. The 360-degree nature of the modern battlefield doesn't exclude anyone from inherent danger. Today there are women on most forward operating bases in both Iraq and Afghanistan, even if only a few, and each of them helps the military run smoothly. I do have an issue with the standards women are required to uphold. I can run faster than a female on the Army fitness test and fail while the female soldier, requiring a lower time, passes. This means we're not judged on a level playing field. If a soldier is wounded in combat and has to be dragged to safety, his fellow soldier should be able to help him out regardless of gender. I think everyone should be judged the same because in combat any person can be asked to do all of the same things. The standard should be made uniform. Women who serve are heroes, just like men who serve, capable of all the same things.

## WHAT VALUES DO YOU FIGHT FOR —CONSERVATIVE OR LIBERAL?

I don't make it a secret that I self identify as a conservative and a Republican. In fact, I'm proud of my political affiliations. That being said I have a great many friends who are very liberal and I love them just the same. When you're in the United States it's easy to argue over every little issue. You have both that luxury as well as that right because men have paid for it in the past with their blood. It's an all-volunteer military force. Nobody was drafted. The truth of the matter isn't all that glamorous though. When you actually take fire you will react not for George W. Bush or Barack Obama. You will react for Private Jones, the guy next to you. You fight for each other because in the heat of the moment that's all you have. You've got your life and the lives of your brothers. Politics and everything else going on in the world dissolves from existence. None of that could be further from your mind. Donkey, elephant, Bull Moose—parties don't mean a thing when you're a target. Also, I can say that I served under both a Republican and a Democrat presidency and did not feel a difference as a soldier serving overseas.

## WHAT'S YOUR OPINION ON THE POTENTIAL REPEAL OF DON'T ASK DON'T TELL?

Eventually the government is going to have to address this issue more seriously than they have in the past. There are homosexuals in the military. There always have been, and I'm sure many do their job well. Change never comes easy. Once upon a time there was strong opposition to raising what would become the 54TH Massachusetts Volunteer Infantry, which ended up being a successful African-American regiment during the Civil War. Look how far we've come. I don't think anyone should have to be more uncomfortable than they have to be, especially in a combat zone. A great many people are uncomfortable serving with homosexuals. There are huge social and religious implications but I have no doubt at all that the future will be one without Don't Ask Don't Tell. You can hate change but you can't do anything to stop it. I'm a heterosexual. I recognize the right of a homosexual person to exist. I do not believe changes should be made in military policies, which have an unknown impact on combat operations while we are fighting wars on multiple fronts. This issue should be addressed after intense combat operations in Iraq and Afghanistan cease. That would be the responsible thing to do. Gender and sexual orientation are not determinate of what makes a good person or soldier, but it's rather a person's character and drive that dictates success in the Armed Forces.

## PEOPLE SEEM TO BE EITHER STRONGLY FOR OR AGAINST OUR OCCUPATION OF IRAQ. HOW DO YOU PREVENT SOUNDING BIAS WHEN YOU SPEAK ABOUT YOUR TIME THERE?

Let's face the fact—everyone has biases. In speaking and in writing I always try to do my best to be honest. In keeping a journal I was able to reference how I felt and what I was personally going through on specific days of my deployment journey—my opinions. I've done my best to paint an accurate picture of my experiences as a support soldier attached to an infantry regiment during the Iraq War. I feel like I've accomplished this goal in a way that is likely very different than any portrayal of modern war that you've read or seen on television. That being said I'm sure that there are times when I showed bias in one way or another. This is something that I grappled with time and again as I began to refine my journal for eventual publication, and as I spoke to different crowds about what I'd endured as a soldier. When I first considered turning my journal into a book I shared my raw, un-edited work with some of the soldiers that I had deployed with. Though most were just excited to be remembered, there were a few who made comments like "that's not how it happened", or "I remember that differently." I'm sure they do. In at least one case, a reader mentioned that my opinion on some subjects seemed to conflict from one paragraph to another. Each of us saw the world and our place in it through a different lens, a different set of eyes. My upbringing, my insecurities, my political leanings, my absolute faith in my God, and my unwavering love for my brothers in arms were all factors that contributed to how I viewed my world and my time in Iraq and Kuwait. Time has a way of changing perceptions. There were many men and women who were better soldiers than I was, but I always viewed myself as a good soldier. So, though my story may not be a perfect candidate for a history textbook, I'd argue that from my perspective it is an extremely honest attempt at a memoir.

### DID YOU CARRY A BIG KNIFE?

Why does everyone ask this question? Am I Crocodile Dundee? I did not carry a knife in the Rambo sense of the word. I carried a small Gerber multi-tool that was useful is taking apart my weapon and opening our field meals, which came in sealed bags. For me there was never an obvious threat of hand-to-hand combat as carrying ample ammunition and moving in teams all but eliminated the chance of Greco-Roman style combat. I did have the opportunity to acquire and mail home several Russian—and Chinese-made bayonets that came off of terrorist AK-47 rifles, but these were mementoes and did not contribute to or take away from my combat effectiveness. My duty weapon was an M-4 rifle, an "assault-style" rife from the M-16 family of firearms. For a time I also carried an M-9 Beretta handgun. There were larger more powerful machine style weapons on every patrol that I took part in.

## WHAT'S IT LIKE COMING HOME?

I am still figuring it out. It's easy and hard all at once. I moved through a wide array of feelings, and started, for me, like this: For the last year you've been making a difference. You have to teach yourself that you're not on the front lines anymore. You have to trick your mind into accepting that when you go to sleep you won't have a sand storm or outgoing artillery "lullaby" to sooth you. It's also lonely. In Iraq we didn't have any alone time at all. I was always with somebody, mostly another sergeant that was my roommate. Living like that makes you close friends but you also have occasional brawls. At first it felt like no one respected what I had accomplished. Very few people can understand what it's like to survive a deployment, far less than one percent of the total population, even fewer do so with the 1-112TH Infantry. When you come home you have to start all over. Unfortunately you can't always start where you left off because some of the people that were major players in your life have already moved on to other things. It can be tough at times. It sucks. The most discouraging thing is the "Kardashians" of popular culture who you all seem to value. I think that people need to be more worthy of the sacrifice made by soldiers. The world is crazy. Earn the sacrifice.

## DO MILITARY LEADERS IMPACT THE POLITICAL ARENA IN THE UNITED STATES?

Yes, but not nearly as much as they should. I am waiting for the day when my fellow soldiers and all of the other people that make up the armed forces of the United States of America will stand up and say, "Enough is enough!" At the same time, veterans make up such a small population that it's difficult for them to impact real change. What's going on right now is criminal. America's finest young men and women are being slaughtered in third world countries and for what? The administration that runs our country appoints politicians and generals from a variety of backgrounds to visit our nation's combat zones. When reports come back, they are ignored. If General McChrystal, General Petraeus, or General Mattis say that we need more troops then give them more troops! If they say they need more equipment then give them more equipment. And if they say they need money then for God's sake don't be stingy. Whatever you do, do not—I repeat do not—ignore the advice of the men on the ground that have the vital insight required to make the best decisions possible! When we do this we are making the same mistakes that claimed lives in past wars. You have to learn from your mistakes. I am not pro-war. I support and love the military as well as my country more than words could ever accurately describe. I joined the Army because it was the right thing to do. For me personally, going to Iraq was the right thing to do as well, if for no other reason than to relieve the men that had already been there for up to 15 month's time. I had no regrets about my decision to enlist in the Armed Forces of the United States. Even so, I do believe that in this age of prolonged nontraditional warfare the best way to support our troops is to bring them home. You can call us a republic or a democracy but no one can deny that America is the new Rome. We are an empire. Our forefathers' fears about the inherent danger of maintaining a standing Army with garrisons all around the globe have been realized. Ideals such as those of honor, glory, and values have been replaced by the power of the dollar—shallow money. I am not an expert on political science or economics but I don't have to be an expert to see the many potential advantages of moving towards a more isolationist mentality. No one can deny that a huge reason for the decline of the American dollar is debt and the concept of fiat money. We've got to stop borrowing and we've got to slow spending. A huge amount of money has gone into the Department of Defense spending budget. So much money has been spent that I once had a college professor, Dr. Koshan, challenge that nobody in a class of nearly one hundred students could find and present an accurate budget for the DOD outlining how much was being spent on the Global War on Terror. In 2005 no one could do it! I'm doubtful that the average person could do it today. This is pathetic! The government is responsible for answering to the people. The President, Congress, and even your local mayor work for you. You don't work for them! It was your vote that put these people in power and it is their responsibility to represent your interest as an American citizen as well as they possibly can.

As for myself getting involved in politics, I have to say that if it happens it happens. As a returning combat veteran, people always ask me what my opinion is on a variety of topics, most of which are about overseas military actions. Every time I open my mouth I feel like I'm telling people things that they have never heard before. The questions I've received have been so overwhelming that it further inspired me to publish my journals here in book form. The problem with the average civilian commenting on the war effort in Iraq is that most of them have never been there. Average people draw their opinions from an American media powerhouse that generally has extreme biases. You cannot learn about the world if you live in a bubble. Though it isn't uncommon to see politicians or even generals on the nightly news, you will seldom, if ever, hear from the private or specialist. Although on one hand you get to hear from the men who make the big decisions, you rarely hear from the grunts that actually have to carry these missions out. I have just as much of a right to my opinion as high-ranking officers do. When I would tell people that the war strategies in both Iraq and Afghanistan were completely inefficient they would generally scowl and cite the declining Allied casualty rate as an example of success.

I cannot understand why a military leader of this or any era would lay out future plans, alert the enemy as to which moves he was going to make and when, then allow time for the enemy to decide on an effective strategy to wait out or react to the coming storm. Make no mistake about it; this is what President Obama did during a December 1, 2009 speech held at the United States Military Academy at West Point, New York. Never tell your enemies your plans.

I can't in good conscience single out Democratic Party leaders for this injustice to U.S. Service members. The Bush administration also had similar press releases, which hurt the average soldier. I think American politicians should be required to read Sun Tzu's *The Art of War*, which highlights ageless tactical philosophy. When playing poker you don't show your opponents your cards, nor should you in war. As a nation I feel that we have grown too soft. New social courtesy requirements force us to become either more aligned with globalization or, as an alternative, more isolationists in a time period where international power, commerce, and responsibilities are virtual requirements for maintaining world power status. A single global economy must be resisted if America is to remain prosperous. We can't have our cake and eat it too. Politicians are not soldiers.

## WHY DID YOU KEEP A JOURNAL?

I kept this journal for many reasons. I wanted to remember my own experiences in Iraq and I wanted to honor all of the men and women that I had the privilege of serving with. My story had heroes like Chad Edmundson, 20, and Mark Baum, 32—soldiers from our brigade who were killed in action, and others like them who are gone but not forgotten. Every person I served with was a true patriot, and a real American hero. We all left our lives behind to go fight in a far off land. American Soldiers, Sailors, Airmen, and Marines continue this proud tradition every day.

I'm sure that there is a lot that I left out. Some things I left out because I forgot, some because it's too personal, and some because I felt like disclosing it might endanger the lives of my brothers who are still fighting. Perhaps if demand is great, I will write a sequel to answer the unanswered questions and fill in any gaps. I kept this journal because I wanted to show everyone what it was like to be a support soldier in a combat unit. In many cases my words could never give the reality due justice.

I ask that if you see a serviceman at church or at the supermarket you approach them, shake their hand and say thank you. Believe me, they'll appreciate it. I also ask that if you see something being done that you believe is wrong, whether it's in life, work, school, or otherwise, that you act on it. Stand up for what you believe in and for your morals. It is the virtue of courage that made America great and it is courage that will sustain us.

I am proud of my service and my military career will continue in a reserve capacity. I miss my brothers from the 112TH every second of every day. Everyday I wake up I think about the guys and I try to live my life in a way that honors them, without fear.

*"The soldier, above all other people, prays for peace, for he must suffer and bear the deepest wounds and scars of war."*

—General Douglas MacArthur

# ABOUT THE AUTHOR

**D**R. WALTER L. ROSADO is the author of *Without Fear* and a decorated U.S. Army combat veteran of overseas military operations under the Global War on Terrorism to include the Iraq Campaign. His military awards include the Army Combat Action Badge and the Army Commendation Medal. Dr. Rosado currently works as a change management consultant for a major healthcare technologies firm. He holds a Ph.D. from Robert Morris University, a M.S. from Duquesne University, and a B.A. from Thiel College. He resides at his home in Pittsburgh, Pennsylvania.

# PHOTOGRAPHS

WALTER ROSADO AT FORT SILL, OKLAHOMA, 2007.

WALTER BATTLED WITH WEIGHT FLUCTUATION FOR MOST OF HIS LIFE AND USED HIS DESIRE TO SERVE HIS COUNTRY AS MOTIVATION TO STAY ON TRACK.

Walter Rosado's Field Artillery Basic Combat Training Class. Fort Sill, Oklahoma 2007.

Rosado (Center) with his squad at Advanced Individual
Training in Fort Jackson SC. 2008.

THE AUTHOR AT HOME FOR LEAVE IN 2008 JUST PRIOR LEAVING
FOR HIS IRAQ DEPLOYMENT.

THE AUTHOR AND OTHER SOLDIERS WAIT TO BOARD THE FLIGHT
FROM McGUIRE AIR FORCE BASE, NEW JERSEY TO KUWAIT.
(PHOTO BY GEORGE DE ESCH)

One of the 1-112th Mine Resistant Armored Personnel Vehicles prepares to embark from Camp Taji.
(Photo by Larry Deal)

THE AUTHOR DUAL WIELDING M16A2 RIFLES AT A FORWARD
OPERATING BASE.

THE AUTHOR POSING FOR A PHOTO WHILE ON "TOWER DUTY"
IN A WATCHTOWER.

THE S-1 SECTION OF HEADQUARTERS 1-112TH INFANTRY REGIMENT IN KUWAIT PRIOR TO PUSHING NORTH INTO IRAQ. STANDING (L TO R): TONY REITZ, JUSTIN ADAMOWICZ, RICHARD GRIFFITH, BENJAMIN SMITH, WALTER ROSADO, MAURICE JASPER. KNEELING (L TO R): BRAD MCDONALD, MATTHEW FASSETTE, CHARLES PEARSON.

A 1-112th Soldier on foot patrol in Iraq. (Photo by Michael Sullivan)

56TH BRIGADE SOLDIERS SECURING A ROOFTOP IN IRAQ. (OFFICIAL U.S. ARMY PHOTO)

THE "TANK GRAVEYARD" AT AL TAJI IRAQ, WHERE THE REMNANTS OF SADDAM HUSSEIN'S CAVALRY RUSTED AWAY UNDER THE HOT SUN.

1-112TH SOLDIERS AND IRAQ ARMY SOLDIERS ON A JOINT AIR
ASSAULT MISSION, BOARDING A UH-60 BLACKHAWK HELICOPTER.
(PHOTO BY MICHAEL SULLIVAN)

1-112TH STRYKERS ON A MOUNTED COMBAT PATROL (CONVOY) NEAR SADR CITY, IRAQ.

1-112-CDR                                                          26 February 2009

MEMORANDUM FOR Commander, 3rd Brigade Combat Team, 82nd Airborne Division

Subject: Request Authorization to Wear the 82nd Airborne Division Shoulder Sleeve Insignia –
Former War Time Service (SSI-FWTS)

1. The 1st Battalion 112th Infantry Stryker Brigade Combat Team was OPCON to the 3rd Brigade
Combat Team, 82nd Airborne Division on or about 6 February 2009 to on or about 11 March
2009.

2. Request that the soldiers on the attached roster be authorized to wear the 82nd Airborne
Division SSI-FWTS IAW ALARACT 055/2007 and AR 670-1, paragraph 28-17.

3. POC for this request is CPT Benjamin B. Smith at benjamin.smith@56bct28id.army.smil.mil
or SVOIP 786-9304.

Encl

27Feb09
FRANCIS T. FLANAGAN
LTC, IN
Commander

THE 1-112TH WAS THE ONLY UNIT IN THE 56TH STRYKER
BRIGADE TO BE OPERATIONAL CONTROL (OPCON) TO THE 3RD
BRIGADE, 82ND AIRBORNE DIVISION. WALTER ROSADO WAS
ONE OF LESS THAN FORTY SOLDIERS TO SERVE WITH THE PARA-
TROOPERS AS A LEG ATTACHMENT AND SOLDIER. HHC 1-112TH
SERVED WITH ELEMENTS FROM THE 82ND AIRBORNE, THE 1ST
CAVALRY DIVISION, AND THE 25TH INFANTRY DIVISION OVER
THE DURATION OF OUR DEPLOYMENT.

The author in front of a Stryker armored personnel carrier vehicle at Camp Taji, Iraq.

56TH BRIGADE SOLDIERS ON FOOT PATROL IN IRAQ. (OFFICIAL U.S. ARMY PHOTO)

A sheik in the 1-112th's Area of Operations (AO) takes a moment to kiss his daughter. (Photo by Michael Sullivan)

The Swords of Qadisiyah, Baghdad, Iraq. (Photo was digitally enhanced/modified for publication)

WALTER ROSADO'S ARMY COMBAT ACTION BADGE. AWARDED FOR
ACTION ON APRIL 12, 2009 FOR "BEING PERSONALLY PRESENT AND
ACTIVELY ENGAGING OR BEING ENGAGED BY THE ENEMY, AND PER-
FORMING SATISFACTORILY IN ACCORDANCE WITH THE PRESCRIBED
RULES OF ENGAGEMENT."

Nick Lehota and Walter Rosado. Nick was an Infantryman that served with Walter in both the 112th and in the
128th. Both were proud to earn the right to wear the
keystone combat patch of the 28th Infantry Division for
service in Iraq, known throughout the military as the
"Bloody Bucket".

The soldiers of the 1-112th Infantry safely back on American soil at Fort Dix, New Jersey. (Photo by Bill Grosinski)

WALTER ROSADO RE-JOINING THE CO-ED 128TH BRIGADE
SUPPORT BATTALION IN PITTSBURGH, PA AFTER RETURNING
HOME FROM IRAQ.

The funeral of SPC Chad Edmundson. Edmundson was one of the soldiers from the 56th Stryker Brigade who was Killed in Action during our 2009 deployment. (Photo by J.D. Cavrich)

THE ORIGINAL SINE TIMORE (WITHOUT FEAR) SCOTTISH HIGH-
LANDER FAMILY CREST PIN, A GIFT TO WALTER ROSADO FROM
MR. WALTON COOK, AND THE INSPIRATION FOR THE TITLE OF
THIS BOOK.